Star-Spangled Kitsch

An Astounding and Tastelessly Illustrated
Exploration of the Bawdy, Gaudy, Shoddy
Mass-Art Culture in This Grand Land of Ours

Curtis F. Brown

UNIVERSE BOOKS
New York

Published in the United States of America in 1975
by Universe Books
381 Park Avenue South, New York, N.Y. 10016
© 1975 by Universe Books

Library of Congress Catalog Card Number: 75-1139
ISBN 0-87663-256-8

Printed in the United States of America

Designed by Harry Chester Associates

Star-Spangled Kitsch

Kitch: Artwork which
is inferior, pretentious
or in bad taste!
Chambers 20th C. dict.

STEVEN

↖ slightly kitchy

Contents

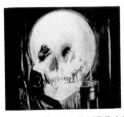

Democratic nations . . . cultivate the arts which serve to render life easy, in preference to those whose object is to adorn it. They will habitually prefer the useful to the beautiful, and they will require that the beautiful should be useful.
—Alexis de Tocqueville, *Democracy in America*

The wrong of unshapely things is a wrong too great to be told.
—William Butler Yeats, "The Lover Tells of the Rose in His Heart"

It's ugly, but is it Art?
—Randall Jarrell, *Pictures from an Exhibition*

CHAPTER 1

Kitsch As Only Kitsch Can

An intrepid introduction to schlock, camp, and kitsch—
American-style

After All, If Kitsch Isn't a Pleasure, Why Bother?

Bonjour, pardner, and a real warm welcome to a wunnerful world of charm and elegance, heart-warming adorableness, and delightfully perverse American ingenuity.

Like it or not, kitsch is the daily, everywhere art of our time, and because we are surrounded by it—in stores and shoppes, in mail-order catalogs, in public events and popular entertainment—we accept it, decry it, or try, probably futilely, to ignore it. If you're a snob, kitsch is the stuff the neighbors collect, not the lovely things that add to the joy and richness of living in *your* gracious home.

First, a ground rule before we begin our Gradus ad Parnassum to the dizzying heights of kitsch at its most flamboyant, most outrageous, and—Heaven help us all—its most lovable. Don't think of kitsch as either "good" art or "bad" art. Most of it hasn't the least idea of being the first, so why should it be labeled, by default, the other? Certainly, kitsch has its grandiose pretensions, its pomposities, its megalomania, even; but its aspirations are not toward what the collective opinion of critics calls Art. Kitsch objects are no more the "opposite" of art than kitsch social phenomena are the counterpart of "nice" norms of behavior or "acceptable" attitudes. Instead, kitsch fills another kind of bill: it feeds the mass appetite for the slick, the sentimental, the sensational, and the supercolossal.

Kitsch need not mean the fall of Western civilization through cultural self-abasement. Like Archibald MacLeish's rationale for a poem, kitsch doesn't *mean*, it only *is*.

Let's begin our Stairway to Paradise with a simple example, a sweat shirt emblazoned with a printed likeness of Leonardo's *Mona Lisa*. Few people are likely to mistake that combination of art and apparel for Art. The buyer is perfectly aware that the decorated shirt is not unique, but a widely available commodity. However, even a sweat shirt, if it bears a picture of a Timeless Masterpiece, not a campy or trendy one of Bugs Bunny or Mick Jagger, can transcend the utilitarian and spell Class.

That is what much of kitsch art generally is, a mass-produced item that its purchaser believes endows him with an air of richness, elegance, or sophistication. (The American art critic Meyer Schapiro wryly defines kitsch as "chic spelled backwards.")

Call kitsch what you will—Crapola or True Elegance (both untrue), or Aesthetic Chutzpah (nearer the truth)—it is as elusive of definition as what constitutes good or bad taste. Whether the sight or experience of kitsch

evokes from you a grin or a groan (Kitsch, *for the smile of pleasure* . . . *Kitsch, for the wince of pain*), let's agree that kitsch can be a victory, however inadvertent or however well or dubiously earned, of form over function.

What else to label, other than "kitsch," Ye Olde Time Potbelly Stove returning as a Handsome Smoking Stand? *Turn-of-the-Century charm revived in an old-fashioned, black cast iron potbelly stove lovingly reproduced in miniature, enhanced by burnished gold highlights, topped by a 10" metal smoker's tray holding an authentic hobnail colored-glass liner. Nearly 2' high, it lends a warmly decorative touch to living room or office. $13.95.*

Aside from its usefulness, such an item fills an aesthetic need in thousands of decent, tax-paying citizens who don't care a snap that they're giving house or office room to a triumph of form over function. It's little they care what "artistic" path an object takes, as long as it looks and acts like value for money. Who cares that the Handsome Smoking Stand is sham? No one drawn to kitsch broods over the fact that it is a counterfeit in which two unrelated objects are blended—or more precisely in this case, screwed and bolted together—into an item that will be eternally at war with itself: a stove that's not really a stove, a smoking stand that isn't simply a smoking stand because part of it is a stove, which isn't really a stove . . .

So we have what is quintessentially a kitsch item, a knockout of a decorative non-stove masquerading as a smoking stand. (Remember, in the world of kitsch, form prevails over function.)

Notice the kitsch pitch of the quoted ad copy. One of the most overworked terms in American kitsch promotion is "old-fashioned," with its folksy air that implies fine craftsmanship. Brothers-under-the-skin-game expressions are "traditional," applied to any piece of furniture stained to look like maple, the all-American prestige wood, and "home-style," which could as easily refer to broken or irregular seconds of cookies or canned peaches. For all its antique charm, just what is a homely potbelly stove doing "enhanced with gold highlights"? The answer is that in the realm of kitsch anything—a beer-can opener, a metallic statuette immortalizing a departed pet, or baby's first shoes—is nicer in bold bronze or glorious gold. Although burnished gold vaguely suggests the old fashioned or traditional, that idea was spawned in some kitschman's imagination. The final sales clincher is the "authentic hobnail colored-glass" ashtray. Authentic to *what*, we wonder.

A college freshman was asked to write a brief essay describing domestic life in the Boston of Hester Prynne. After some careful detailing of contemporary dress, household furnishings, and mode of speech, the student let his fancy roam and introduced a visitor into his hypothetical family circle. When his hostess asked the guest what he would take by way of refreshment, he replied, "A glass of iced tea." (A relapsed Puritan might have requested another summertime cooler, perhaps a Pink Lady.) Although the writer did not record that the tea was poured over ice cubes, he reported that it was served with something sounding faintly in period, a plate of hickory toast.

Riffle through any recent mail-order house catalog, one of those cornucopias bursting with Exciting New Ideas, and chances are you'll find a kitsch item the mistress of that 17th-century house may have used (had the student pressed ahead with his particulars) to prevent unsightly moisture rings on her table. *Join the Colonial American Set With Authentic-Style Coasters!* runs the kitsch catalog blurb. *Be proud of that eagle emblem on smart cork-lined coasters housed in a wood-grain Colonial stack-pack 5" high. Guests will thrill to the traditional mood you set as they admire these 8 plastic coasters that will not chip or mar. $1.98.*

If the castiron potbelly stove and smoking stand (22") doesn't warm your heart, try a plaster potbelly stove table lamp with an eagle decal on the shade. For something a little more traditional, get yourself a real potbelly stove, paint it white with a little gold here and there, and plant philodendron or—if you're a snob—ivy.

For the moment, never mind the unaccountably rococo handle attached to the coaster pack; ignore the anachronism of a *pre*-revolutionary eagle motif printed on the cork lining of each coaster (kitsch bric-a-brac, from coasters to toilet-seat covers, is obsessed with the American eagle, as are presumably its multitude of customers). Contemplate instead the when-eras-collide elements that qualify the item as kitsch. Both the case and the coasters are hexagonal, a shape that kitsch designers equate with Dignity. A diminutive drawer, decorated with an applied brass-toned post-revolutionary eagle pull to sustain the "colonial" theme, is set in into the base. Of course—just the thing to hold antique plastic hors-d'oeuvres picks!

Here again is the kitsch inversion of values in which utility yields to pretentious form, this time accented by an eagle, one of the OK-trappings of anything aspiring to authentic Americana. Conclusion: "traditional" patriotic coasters, however historically impossible, are preferable to ordinary attractive ones.

But then, what are years when you're Talking Colonial Iced-drink Accessories, crafted of plastic?

Perhaps that imaginative student, whose visitor from the "Twilight Zone" evinced a presentiment of a liquor never brewed, is today a proud member of the Colonial American Set as his guests thrill to the traditional mood provided by eight authentic-style colonial coasters.

The delights of passing through the kitsch time warp aren't limited to stay-at-homes. Fortunately, at every hand are helpful columnists in local magazines and newspapers. As long as there are restaurants for them to discover and gush over, Americans on the move need never hunger for kitsch.

Authentic colonial cocktail coasters of plastic and cork (6½"). The drawer is indispensable for holding hors-d'oeuvres picks for those early American pickled herring tidbits and party franks. The clash of function and material, and the style of decorative elements are marks of classic kitsch.

The Eager Eater
The Auto-crat of the Dinner Table
A LIBERTY BELL OF FARE

Be sure to set aside one of these snapcrackle days full of autumn's giddyingly golden glory for a gastronomic gala that will have *toute la famille* pinching itself in disbelief for months. I can't think of a better way to sit out winter's discontent than in rapturous retrospect of a Sunday dinner at what could well be my favorite restaurant hereabouts, The Federalist Flagon.

While the sere and yellow leaves are still with us, flee the big city and head northward on Route 22. (It's *your* day, so poke along at an eye-feasting 35 mph.) Turn off at 22A, savor the rustic splendor for a mile or so, and behold!—you're at the sign of the Double-F. (Inspired thoughtfulness recently prompted Mine Host to open the so *very* practical Spirit of '76 Car-Wash across the way. Dine and shine, you might say.)

Remember, it's fun all the way as you're welcomed at the door by a maître d' who's got up as a Tory-loving Hessian mercenary. No waiting—he'll march you right to your table of good, stout oak, where your order will be taken by one of the colorfully costumed Betsy Rossettes, as briskly efficient a brigade of bustling waitresses as you'll find this side of Mount Vernon.

I've been tipped that the most-requested family meal consists of Colonial Fruite Cuppe, with a dab of cranberry (but *naturally*) sherbet; Tuna Ticonderoga, a scrumptious creamed dish served within a "stockade" of potato sticks; and Abigail's Ambrosia, a mouth-slavering medley of batter-coated peas and carrots.

For dessert, set your tricorns for jaunty portions of Valley Forge Freeze, a confection of hand-crushed ice and maraschino cherries. (General Washington's boys should have had it so good!) Let your Littlest Rebels wash it all down with flagonettes (keep 'em, they're on the house) of bubbly Boston Harbor Punch. You grownups can slosh it up with Early American-style draft beer, served at room temperature in pewter Molly Pitchers.

At only $6.50 a freedom-loving head, who's going to complain to George III?

With Bicentennial time here, you'll want to light your torch and prove your devotion to liberty and those other qualities that have made America great. If I find a better way to stand up and be counted than a visit to The Federalist Flagon, I'll let you know.

Kitsch breaks the time-barrier! Kitsch lives!

★ ★

And You Thought That One Man's Kitsch Was Another Man's Schlock

To state a simple fact simply, about the only thing we know etymologically of the term "kitsch" is that it is a German colloquialism for—face it—trash or rubbish.

However, a kitsch buff should be wary of blurred nomenclature. Kitsch is definitely not to be confused with schlock, which really is simple-minded junk, from party pepper-uppers to cheap ("modestly priced") decorative items. ("Schlock," a Yiddish word—from the German *Schlag*, a sudden hit or blow—originally meant "damaged goods" at a cheap price.)

Rooting around at the bottom of the schlock bin, pull out a few basic examples: a statuette of a tuxedoed, bleary-eyed, and red-nosed drunk embracing a pliant lamppost; a rude noisemaker to be placed under toilet-seat assemblies for the mutual merriment of convulsed host and embarrassed guest *(Installs easily on the throne; it's durable and it's sanitary)*; condoms affixed to roguish greeting cards, and a thousand more Zany Gags Good for a Million Laughs. Healthy Chaucerian bawdry those schlock items may be, as their literate apologists maintain; other opinions regard them as subjective inanities intended only to amuse or disgust, or both.

Willie the Weeper (7¾") weewees when you pull down his shorts. When you pat the bald head of the Naughty Monk (7½"), an erection emerges. Bawdy jokes and gimcracks are a kind of unpretentious schlock, and date from the time man first learned to laugh at himself.

The upper layers of the schlock barrel produce a new and cheaply turned out reproduction of an 18th-century "Dresden" shepherdess figurine, the exquisite detail and delicate tinting of a period original coarsened, blunted, or missing altogether; a couple of plush wall-hangings, one so blatantly a crude rendering of *The Last Supper* as to be blasphemous, the other a barely recognizable representation of the Capitol at Washington; and a display plate that keeps ever green a memory of the Eugene, Oregon, skyline. These articles, though on a relatively loftier level than that of Jack's Joke Shop paraphernalia, possess an uncomplicated straightforwardness and so remain schlock, whatever tender or reverent sentiments they may strive to arouse in the beholder.

Most people's eyes abhor a vacuum, and it is for many of them that the large schlock market exists. Schlock accumulators are tempted on every hand by "minniquins" of a slightly sexy Virgin Mary, Michelangelo's *David*, and the *Venus de Milo* (Masterpieces You'll Be Proud Of), all rendered in a lard-like plastic substance suggesting the flesh of a cadaver. Those schlock items are of real value only to their manufacturers as evidence of what impulse-buyers will grab up, at minimum outlay, to dignify the odd shelf or corner.

A schlock fancier, equating unfilled living space with poverty or insensibility to Life's Finer Things, blankets mantelpieces, table tops, and wall areas with a donkey clearly delighted to be drawing a cactus-sprouting cart; a Nubian slave languidly supporting a lamp; a scattering of prim and pasty figurines of small children; and Gainsborough's *Blue Boy*, Millet's *The Gleaners*, and El Greco's *View of Toledo*, advertised as "reproduced in the same luxurious full-color of the priceless originals," but in reality printed in cyanotic blues, insipid pinks, and murky browns.

The schlock collector wants not so much Things in Good Taste as he wants Nice Things in Nice Taste. At the same time, he feels he must convey the impression that only thrift or humble means prevent him from showing an even grander display of interesting objects and deceptive copies of museum originals. Thus, he settles prudently for the immediate appeal of a kerchiefed tot perched in the crotch of a blossoming apple tree, or for wretchedly printed reproductions and vile miniature replicas that he believes to be only a notch away from The Real Thing.

Times and customs change, and the world is not as it was. The Golden Age of schlock reached its apogee in the gewgaw-strewn Victorian parlor, stuffed with schlock objects for stuffing's own sweet sake. The only slightly diminished urge to accumulate characterless knickknacks survives into our Silver Age of schlock. Today's home furnishers, bent on enhancing their surroundings with fewer but more ambitiously conceived art objects, appear to be more discriminating. Painstaking perusal of well-supplied novelty emporiums, gift shoppes, and mail-order catalogs suggests it is up-and-doing kitsch, not ho-hum schlock, that is finding a place in the hearts and homes of America.

To understand how kitsch goes further than schlock to do a bigger job, compare a garish cotton-and-rayon tapestry memorializing the assassinated Dr. Martin Luther King, Jr. and the Kennedy brothers with a glass ashtray bearing photographic transfers of the two Kennedys. Are both kitsch? The wall hanging decorates and commemorates. But the ashtray? Kitsch, the Irrepressibly Articulate, pipes up loud and clear: *Come on, folks, stub out*

GETS YOU TO THE CHURCH ON TIME.

BULOVA ACCUTRON
For men and women

Now is the time for the Good Book to come to the aid of the watch industry. For openers, an adaptation of a lyric from *My Fair Lady*, then a dash of Ecclesiastes ("to every thing there is a season and a time to every purpose under the heaven"), and a pinch of the Twenty-third Psalm's "paths of righteousness." Within a few precisely measured seconds, Madison Avenue mingles Holy Writ with Broadway.

your cigarettes and cigars right into the upturned, inspiring faces of our martyred New York State Senator, Robert F. Kennedy (1925-1968), and his brother John F. Kennedy (1917-1963), thirty-fifth President of the United States of America!

No harm is intended by the manufacturer of that kitsch artifact. Just put it down to a lapse in judgment and not seeing a chilling discrepancy between the pious aim and the off-putting result.

Another, classic example of absurd juxtaposition of kitsch of that sort comes from England in an advertising jingle:

> Hark! the herald angels sing
> Beecham's Pills are just the thing!
> Peace on earth and mercy mild,
> Two for man and one for child.

The mingling of a carol celebrating the birth of Christ with the huckstering of a drug to stimulate evacuation of the bowels haunted Sir Thomas Beecham, son of the successful laxative manufacturer, throughout a distinguished career as a symphony and opera conductor.

We see now that kitsch may embody not only the Alliance Uneasy (ye olde timey, gold-burnished stove and smoking stand combo) and the Dream Impossible (coasters just like the ones our colonial forefathers used) but also the Gaffe Gruesome (matches, ashes, and smelly ground-out butts for murdered national leaders).

Kitsch goes beyond dull schlock—all the way to shudder-making shock!

Is It Kitsch or Is It Camp?

Camp is another broad category that should be combed out from the rich fabric of kitsch. A useful rule of thumb: Kitsch rarely intends to be frivolous; camp usually does.

Kitsch may be ludicrous in its attempts to impress the naive, but humor is not its goal. If it arrives there at all—by detours around the norm in taste or preposterous breaches in chronology, for example—it is inadvertent. Camp solicits the appreciative giggle, courts it, then wrestles it to earth. Although both kitsch and camp may evoke the rapturous response "It's not to be believed!" kitsch is blissfully unaware of being anything but appealing and desirable. Camp, however, offers incongruities in glorious self-awareness.

A model of camp at its highest, or most elegant, is the celebrated scene from Congreve's *The Way of the World*, in which the fine-mannered Millamant and Mirabell lay down their stringent conditions for marriage. The provisos are of so boorish a nature expressed in language of such refinement that the effect is one of delicious inconsistency.

In short, camp mocks bad taste; kitsch exploits it.

Camp arouses our sense of the ridiculous and we respond with amused tolerance. When we see Bette Davis or Ruth Gordon, fine if sometimes flamboyant performers, relax their self-discipline and overextend their acting technique in a superfluity of ineffective gestures—finger-twitching and hip-switching, hand-rubbing or tongue-protruding—we label the sum total as camp. Mae West, whose nasally provocative delivery, eye-rolling, lip-pursing, and pelvic tics parody the conventional invitation to dalliance, is never out of control and is camp, pure and simple. ("I was never pure and I ain't so simple"—one can improvise a campy West-ern put-down.) Camp was also the stock-in-trade of Carmen Miranda, whose retina-searing Techni-

Had Mae West, like Maria Montez, regarded herself as a love goddess, she would rival that Queen of Technicolor Kitsch. Instead, the Queen of Camp chose to spoof sex, showing us that it could be delightfully ludicrous as well as wittily lubricious. Here is the redoubtable enchantress in her classic stage creation, *Diamond Lil* (1928).

In *Cobra Woman* (1944), Montez's straight-faced siren fizzled rather than sizzled.

color get-ups, skyscraper headdresses bearing a season's fruit harvest, clomping platform shoes, and garbled English projected in a voice that could be heard on Mars all came together beautifully in her campy personification of Exaggeration. Had we been blessed with the Brazilian Bombshell's own blazing interpretation of Joan of Arc, the grotesque, if fascinating, result would surely have been kitsch.

The appeal of kitsch to the emotions results in more than showy acquisitiveness and susceptibility to awe. It prods us beyond simple, nostalgic yearnings and sentimentality to irrational acceptance of the impossible or the incongruous—the "antique-colonial" aura of the practical coasters and the tender-cruel reminder of the assassinated Kennedy brothers that doubles as an ashtray. The camp response addresses itself mainly to the intellect; it is content with the risibility of recognition. Observing those two objects, we may laugh at their intrinsic ridiculousness. But the kitsch sensibility rationalizes the appearance of the items. Of the early American coaster set, it says, "The way we were must have been better; after all, aren't most things going from bad to worse?" Of the ashtray, it says, "I remember, I remember."

Camp generates cerebration. For kitsch, the heart has its own reasons and they are enough.

As a perfect example of the kitsch-or-camp quandary, consider the Edsel, an American automobile extravaganza of the late 1950s, born of the Ford Motor Company, soon dead of neglect at the uneager hands of the public.

The car was even more bloated in appearance than most of the other bulging, chrome-covered, accessory-laden American autos of its time; it assembled all the enticing elements of the others into one ponderous whole. It was longer, more needlessly overpowered, more gadget cluttered, more encumbered with expensive accessories than other cars in its medium-price class.

Proclaimed as the heir to the accumulated engineering savvy of the past and the latest wisdom to be collected from the new research techniques in the consumer motivation field, the Edsel was to be not only the best real car but also an embodiment of the dream car already existing in the minds of prospective buyers.

The designers of the Edsel, canny kitsch peddlers in their way, may have figured that if cars are an American sex symbol, an innovative grill design, suggestive of the female genitalia, might make their new product even more desirable. Instead, the distinctive, puckered grill prompted jeering public

In the 1940s, Carmen Miranda brought her brand of flamboyant camp to south-of-the-border musical films such as *Down Argentine Way*, *That Night in Rio*, and *Weekend in Havana*. Often wrongly identified as kitsch, the zany "Brazilian Bombshell" avoided dead-earnest pretention; she never confused her baubles, bangles, and bare midriff with Art.

Would even the names for the Edsel that Marianne Moore came up with have helped this elephant to fly? Arcenciel, Resilient Bullet, and Andante con Moto (a kind of make haste slowly) were among the tags the famous poet suggested. It's doubtful that any name, however catchy, would have put the clumsy kitsch-car of the fifties in many American driveways.

comment, from "It looks like an Olds that sucked a lemon," to more obvious remarks.

The powers at Ford can hardly be said to have come up deliberately with a camp object, although that's what the Edsel has mistakenly been called. But they did produce and market a kitsch item derided in some quarters and avoided by the public where it counted most, in dealers' showrooms. The Edsel (1957-60) was probably the most expensive kitsch article ever offered American consumers—it cost an estimated $250 million to conceive, design, produce, publicize, distribute, and advertise. Americans may have wanted some or all of the Edsel's features, but they didn't want the lumpy leviathan.

It's not hard to see why the Edsel failed so monumentally to prove the answer to the auto-buyer's dream. Even before the car sailed into showrooms it was bombarded by a continuous volley of merciless jokes and sank in a sea of laughter. Kitsch is gobbled up by a public hungry for approval and for things that at least *sound* elegant. Perhaps one of the pretentiously far-out, kitschy names—Mongoose Civique, Dearborn Diamante, Utopian Turtletop—suggested by poet Marianne Moore, whom the company took on as consultant, would have tickled the fancy of consumers. But "Edsel," from the Ford family's scion whose name the company felt had "personal dignity," produced very little music and absolutely no vibes to groove on.

Kitsch aims always at flattering the owner. The Edsel, The Kitsch That Failed, only made him the object of ridicule. The camp-follower, by contrast, good-naturedly invites laughter. When a Volkswagen owner refers to his car as "The Bug," he's self-mockingly deprecating his possession. By attaching an imitation Rolls-Royce grill to the front of the car, he's only pretending that he has made it classy.

The Edsel didn't make it as the car All-America was supposed to want. But as chrome-plated kitsch, ostentatious and grotesque, the Edsel Made It Big.

Kitsch is Instant Dinosaurism!

A Crash Course in Kit. Lit.; or, Grandiose Ineptitude, The Name is Kitsch

If, as Dr. Johnson observed, "Parnassus has its flowers of transient fragrance, as well as its oaks of towering height," then one of the hardiest blossoms blowing on the rugged slopes of that peak consecrated to Apollo and the Muses hallows the memory of Julia A. Moore, known to herself as "The Sweet Singer of Michigan" and to posterity as "The World's Worst Poet."

America's lesser literary fry will never roam with Mrs. Moore the sacred grove of kitsch. Even yesterday's Edgar A. Guest or today's Rod McKuen, for example, are poetasters whose reach, unlike The Sweet Singer's, not once exceeds their grasp. But Homer could nod, and so let us grant an afternoon's nap to eminent men of letters such as Ralph Waldo Emerson and Edgar Allan Poe; and to Thomas Holley Chivers, Congressman Harry C. Canfield, and Don Blanding, a lifelong literary snooze.

The best poetry may be said to set a bronze gong reverberating through the labyrinths of the imagination. Instead, kitsch poetry produces the less resonant clink of spoon on saucepan, either because the writer's muse withheld inspiration temporarily or indefinitely, or because the poet absented himself awhile from a sense of the ridiculous.

An alarming passage from "Alphonse of Castile," possibly Emerson's most sweepingly ecological work, suggests a grisly, Nietzschean Final Solution to the population explosion:

> Earth, crowded, cries: "Too many men!"
> My counsel is, kill nine in ten,
> And bestow the shares of all
> On the remnant decimal.

That is a pessimist's Olympian view of mankind; but from the Sage of Concord—poet, philosopher, and clergyman—the passage is a momentary lapse in taste that earns it a place on Mount Kitsch, if only at its foot.

Poe, who rarely regarded himself a source of unbuttoned jollity, could produce a poem that, although no less inspired than most hymns of the Strife O'er, Battle Won variety, yet rises to a respectable level of literary kitsch. Like a giggle at a funeral, the last line's inadvertent pun shatters the lugubrious mood of this excerpt from "For Annie":

> Thank heaven! the crisis—
> The danger is past
> And the lingering illness
> Is over at last—
> And the fever called "Living"
> Is conquer'd at last.
>
> Sadly, I know,
> I am shorn of my strength,
> And no muscle I move
> As I lie at full length—
> But no matter—I feel
> I am better at length.

Thomas Holley Chivers (1809-58), like William Carlos Williams a century later, was both poet and physician. Unlike Dr. Williams, whose literary accomplishment was considerable, the gentleman from Georgia produced for the most part utter nonsense, under the impression that he was as great a poet, if not greater, than Poe. It's possible that a gemologist might revel in the following exercise in kitsch grotesquery, but all of us would agree that the anticlimactic proper name lacks the ring of fine crystal:

> Many mellow Cydonian suckets,
> Sweet apples, anthosmial, divine,
> From the ruby-rimmed beryline buckets,
> Star-gemmed, lily-shaped, hyaline:
> Like the sweet golden goblet found growing
> On the wild emerald cucumber-tree,
> Rich, brilliant, like chrysoprase glowing,
> Was my beautiful Rosalie Lee.

In "To Allegra Florence in Heaven," Chivers compares, with dogged determination, the torment of a lost love to the fate of Humpty Dumpty. The

Julia A. Moore, "The Sweet Singer of Michigan," aspired to High Seriousness. But an unfaltering instinct for inept detail and badly rhymed bathos and banality made her instead America's High Priestess of kitsch poetry.

result places high among the most ineptly grandiose similes in American literature:

> As an egg, when broken, never
> Can be mended, but must ever
> Be the same crushed egg forever—
>   So shall this dark heart of mine!
> Which, though broken, is still breaking,
> And shall nevermore cease aching
> For the sleep which has no waking—
>   For the sleep which now is thine!

In the course of his suspenseful "Elegy on the Loss of U.S. Submarine S4, Congressman Canfield (1875-1945, D.-Ind., and a Baptist) permits himself a striking slip in Christian charity when he generously pardons, while damning faintly, the doomed crew's last gallant salute to Lady Luck:

> Entrapt inside a submarine,
> With death approaching on the scene,
> The crew compose their minds to dice,
> More for the pleasure than the vice.

Julia A. Moore (1847-1920), prompted by a muse only distantly related to the one who inspired Homer, Dante, and Milton, struggled mightily and valiantly to create grand works on large themes. ("Literary is a work very difficult to do," she reminded her detractors in characteristic style.) In taking contemporary calamities—the Chicago Fire and other Midwestern holocausts, and local instances of infant mortality—as her most compatible province, she gave more heed to her muse than it probably expected. With a will of iron and an ear of tin, Mrs. Moore produced "Ashtabula Disaster," a kitsch collision between high seriousness and misjudged effect that transforms her, Daphne-like, into Dr. Johnson's "oak of towering height" along the upper reaches of Mount Kitsch.

The poem is a painfully limping, shamelessly sentimental account of an accident that occurred a century ago in Ashtabula, a city on Lake Erie in Ohio. Details the poet neglects to provide the reader for a fuller comprehension of the tragedy and its setting include the facts that the Ashtabula River divides the city with a deep ravine and that the bridge spanning the gorge gave way on December 29, 1876.

Mrs. Moore's enthusiasm for dispatching souls onward and upward prompts her to exaggerate the number thus "saved." Of the 156 travelers aboard the train that plummeted 75 feet to unfriendly waters below, a "mere" 85 perished. Among the lost was an evangelist named Philip Paul Bliss who, with Ira D. Sankey, an eminent preacher, published hymns such as "Hold the Fort" and, prophetically for Bliss, "Pull for the Shore." (The opening half-dozen or so lines of "Ashtabula Disaster" anticipate Bobbie Gentry's "Ode to Billie Joe," a popular ballad of a few years ago.)

> Have you heard of the dreadful fate
>   Of Mr. P. P. Bliss and wife?
> Of their death I will relate,
>   And also others lost their life;
> Ashtabula Bridge disaster,
>   Where so many people died
> Without a thought that destruction
>   Would plunge them 'neath the wheel of tide.

The gruesomely embellished gravestone of Jabez Bradbury, Esq., who "departed this life The 13 of January *A.D.* 1781, in the 89th year of his age," still stands in a burial ground in Newburyport, Mass., a grim reminder of the reality of death. Contrast with the monuments in Forest Lawn, where death has evaporated into a twilight-zone gallery of beautiful people.

Old times in new bottles.
Colonial Williamsburg, complete with guides in 18th-century costume, is what Ada Louise Huxtable has dubbed the "pickling" of the past. But not quite. The Capitol is merely an educated guess at what the original building might have looked like. Surrounded by period survivals, however, it passes for authentic early American. Here, the harmony of line, shape, and texture of the handsome, albeit synthetic, building are brutally ill-served by distorted rendering into a bourbon bottle. (10")

Turning antique dry sinks into incongruous hiding places for liquor and entertainment components (both presumably shameful by puritan American standards) depleted the supply of authentic pieces. Even kitschier is the "Yorktown," which, simulates the old kitchen sink, moves to the den, surrounds itself with checkered-tablecloth wallpaper and draperies, and becomes a television set.

The miniaturization of Michelangelo's *Pietà* (10"), thoughtfully labeled so the neighbors know you have culture, epitomizes schlock. The kitsch travesty (5½"), revealing what Michelangelo could have achieved if he'd had his wits about him, enhances the original with gold paint, a blue mirror, and a tin fence. The pathos is turned to Grand Guignol with the addition of Jesus' dripping wounds.

No one would—or is intended to—mistake this Volkswagen, cheerfully camped up with a mock Rolls-Royce grill, for the More Expensive Brand.

Chorus:
Swiftly passed the engine's call,
Hastening souls on to death,
Warning not one of them all;
It brought despair right and left.

Among the ruins are many friends,
   Crushed to death amidst the roar,
On one thread all may depend,
   And hope they've reached the other shore.

P. P. Bliss showed great devotion
   To his faithful wife, his pride,
When he saw that she must perish
   He died a martyr by her side.
P. P. Bliss went home above—
   Left all friends, earth, and fame,
To rest in God's holy love;
   Left on earth his work and name.
The people love his work by numbers,
   It is read by great and small,
He by it will be remembered,
   He has left it for us all.

His good name from time to time
   Will rise on land and sea;
It is known in distant climes,
   Let it echo wide and free.
One good man among the number,
   Found sweet rest in a short time,
His weary soul may sweetly slumber
   Within the vale, heaven sublime.

Destruction lay on every side,
   Confusion, fire and despair;
No help, no hope, so they died,
   Two hundred people over there.
Many ties was there broken,
   Many a heart was filled with pain,
Each one left a little token,
   For above they live again.

In *Following the Equator*, Mark Twain provides a workable definition of kitsch poetry when he remarks that Mrs. Moore afforded "the same deep charm for me that *The Vicar of Wakefield* has, and I find in it the same subtle touch—the touch that makes an intentionally humorous episode pathetic and an intentionally pathetic one funny."

One of The Sweet Singer's finest moments demonstrates her intuitive grasp of the principle of synaesthesia, or confusion of the senses, a vivid literary device often used by symbolist poets and their disciples such as Poe, Rimbaud, T. S. Eliot, and Hart Crane. Mrs. Moore's couplet runs:

> Come all good people, far and near,
> Oh, come and see what you can hear.

Although she enjoyed a wide following in her time, lines like those displeased her critics. The conclusion of "The Author's Early Life" encourages the faithful and scolds the scoffers:

> And now kind friends, what I have wrote,
>   I hope you will pass o'er,
> And not criticise as some have done,
>   Hitherto herebefore.

During the 1930s, "Tony Wons's Scrapbook" was a popular morning radio program. Wons's romantic and intimate voice, wafted from the Stromberg-Carlson, enthralled housewives as they went about washing laundry in Super Suds, preparing whipped lime Jell-O and custard sauce for that evening's dessert, and seeing that the kids got their daily dose of good-tastin' Ovaltine for stronger bodies. A poem that Wons often intoned over the air waves, and which never failed to make the homemakers weak in the knees, was Don Blanding's "Vagabond House," a protracted paean to domestic self-indulgence.

The poem describes a "dream house" fitted out with such a profusion of exotic, mind-boggling trappings and amenities (including a paper knife that "once slit the throat of a Rajah's wife" and cuisine offering rather dubious menus of "curious soups and odd ragouts") that the effect is overwhelmingly cloying—a supremely kitsch dwelling that is both recklessly rich and triumphantly gaudy.

When I have a house . . . as I sometime may . . .
I'll suit my fancy in every way.
I'll fill it with things that have caught my eye
In drifting from Iceland to Molokai.
It won't be correct or in period style,
But . . . oh, I've thought for a long, long while
Of all the corners and all the nooks,
Of all the bookshelves and all the books,
The great big table, the deep, soft chairs,
And the Chinese rug at the foot of the stairs;
It's an old, old rug from far Chow Wan
That a Chinese princess once walked on.

                                           •   •   •   •

And there where the shadows fall I've planned
To have a magnificent Concert Grand
With polished wood and ivory keys
For wild discordant rhapsodies,
For wailing minor Hindu songs,
For Chinese chants and clanging gongs,
For flippant jazz and for lullabies
And moody things that I'll improvise
To play the long gray dusk away
And bid good-by to another day.

Pictures—I think I'll have but three;
One in oil, of a wind-swept sea
With the flying scud and the waves whipped white—
(I know the chap who can paint it right)
In lapis blue and a deep jade green—
A great big smashing fine marine
That'll make you feel the spray in your face—
I'll hang it over my fireplace.

The second picture—a freakish thing—
Is gaudy and bright as a macaw's wing—
An impressionistic smear called "Sin,"
A nude on a striped zebra skin
By a Danish girl I knew in France.
My respectable friends will look askance
At the purple eyes and the scarlet hair,
At the pallid face and the evil stare
Of a sinister, beautiful vampire face.
I shouldn't have it about the place,
But I like—while I loathe—the beastly thing,
And that's the way one feels about sin.

The picture I love best of all
Will hang alone on my study wall
Where the sunset's glow and the moon's cold gleam
Will fall on the face and make it seem
That the eyes in the picture are meeting mine,
That the lips are curved in the fine, sweet line
Of that wistful, tender, provocative smile
That has stirred my heart for a wondrous while.
It's the sketch of a girl who loved too well
To tie me down to that bit of Hell
That a drifter knows when he finds he's held
By the soft, strong chains that passions weld.

 •   •   •   •

I'll have a cook that I'll name Oh Joy,
A sleek, fat, yellow-faced Chinese boy
Who can roast a pig or mix a drink
(You can't improve on a slant-eyed Chink).

 •   •   •   •

Pewter and bronze and hammered brass,
Old carved wood and gleaming glass,
Candles in polychrome candlesticks,
And peasant lamps in floating wicks,
Dragons in silk on a Mandarin Suit,
In a chest that is filled with vagabond loot;
All of the beautiful, useless things
That a vagabond's aimless drifting brings. . . .

As long as conventional sentiments and commonplace insights well up in the breasts of the Aunt Tillies and Uncle Fuds of this world, the kitsch poet, like the poor, will always be with us.

> *Infected by a measly muse*
> *Who rashly makes them itch,*
> *The poets scratch, emote, effuse,*
> *And what they write is Kitsch!*

This Is My Beloved, a best-selling cycle of love poems after the manner of the *Song of Songs* and the *Rubáiyát of Omar Khayyám*, was considered steamy (but tasteful) stuff when it first appeared in 1943. Lines such as "Barked poplars growing out of the dark-matted jungle of her crotch" and "What enslaving cocktail have I sucked from your full mouth . . . to leave me so totally yours!" anticipate an assembly-line style like that of today's Rod McKuen, a mode that might be described as Hallmark's Darker Side.
People would be nicer if, like Jonathan Livingston Seagull, they'd rise above their humdrum conformist nature and acquire instead "a higher purpose for life." For all its modish plumage, Richard Bach's kitsch pop parable is the same old wing-flapping as *The Little Engine That Could* and Longfellow's "The Psalm of Life."

A Guide to Do-It-Yourself Kit.Krit.

"Mike Hammer," Mickey Spillane's hard-boiled private eye, Charles M. Schultz's *Peanuts*, everyman's Marilyn Monroe, and Alfred Hitchcock's less-than-best movies, such as *Vertigo* and *The Birds*, are enormously popular. To the kitsch critic, the more far-out and "heavy" an explanation the better it accounts for the mass appeal of best-selling but mediocre novelists, clever and lovable comic strips, maximally endowed but minimally gifted superstars, and superbly entertaining but absurdly overinterpreted film directors. The more pretentious the critique, the kitschier it is.

Although kitsch criticism is intoxicatingly rich in potential, it is completely mechanical and operates by a basic formula. Step One: Set forth the most preposterous claim for your subject that you can conceive of. Step Two: Bewilder your reader with a razzle-dazzle of esoteric quotations and allusions to support your argument. Step Three: Mix and toss, toss and mix in a

Commentators muster all the critical armament at their command to justify to man the ways of a film artist's lesser achievements. *The Birds* (1963) was Alfred Hitchcock's attempt at an apocalyptic vision. But no amount of kitsch criticism can explain away the distracting, if ingenious, special effects, which swamped the intention.

zesty dressing of arcane jargon borrowed from literary criticism or, for an up-to-date approach, social science catch phrases—for example, Social Darwinism and Left-anarcho-liberalism.

Alternate methods: If your subject is a current rage but shallow, you can either transform faults into virtues or concentrate on style. Insist that Andy Warhol's film *Sleep* is *supposed* to be boring. With practice, you can combine the two methods. For example, assert that Kurt Vonnegut Jr.'s cardboard characters make him a master of "thin characterization" and proclaim that he is the greatest stylist of the American novel.

With these few ground rules in mind, you're ready to play Kitsch Kriticism, a kind of literary miniature golf.

Thou, the Fury: Mickey Spillane's *I, the Jury*, John Donne's "The Good-Morrow," and Existentialism

In Chapter Nine of *I, the Jury*, Mickey Spillane, whose deceptively flat style mirrors perfectly the existential *Angst* of alienated 20th-century man, creates a moment of jarring incongruity that summons up images of both Dante's vision of the transfigured Beatrice of the *Paradiso* and Spenser's Bower of Blisse in *The Faërie Queene*. Mike Hammer, whose name suggests both archangel and scourge of God, stands before the nude Charlotte, who is about to enter the shower (baptism and purification), with two highballs he has just "whipped up," an extension of the hero-as-scourge metaphor.

At that point in the action, metaphysical images, those opposites yoked by violence together, in Dr. Johnson's phrase, erupt in a manner that cannot fail to put the perceptive reader in mind of John Donne's finest poetry. (It is worth noting that in a sly inversion of sensibilities, Spillane introduces the passage with a contrapuntal slant reference to the hot-cold juxtaposition associated with Petrarch's love poems: "When I saw her beautiful body that way my blood boiled inside me and the drink shook in my hand.") In a hitherto unobserved echo of Donne, Spillane's perfect pastiche of neo-Platonism re-creates and makes relevant that other supreme stylist's "The Good-Morrow."

"Both of us finished [the drinks] in one draught. It added nothing to the fire that was running through me. I felt like reaching out and squeezing her to pieces. We put the glasses down on the dresser top. We were awfully close then. One of those moments." (*"My face in thine eye, thine in mine appears,/ And true plain hearts do in the faces rest."*)

Mickey Spillane's soft-porn, hard-boiled novels—for example, *I, the Jury* and *Kiss Me Deadly*—are simplistic kitsch reductions of the fine murder-thriller art of Dashiell Hammett and Raymond Chandler. In *Ring of Fear* (1954), the author portrayed a character not unlike Mike Hammer, the ruthless hero of his novels.

"She came into my arms with a rush, burying her face in my neck. I tilted her head back and kissed her eyes. Her mouth opened for me and I kissed her, hard. I knew I was hurting her, but she didn't pull away. She returned that kiss with her lips, her arms and her body. She was on fire too, trying desperately to get close to me through space that wasn't there any more." (*"For love all love of other sights controls/ And makes one little room an everywhere."*)

"I had my arm around her shoulders and my hands fastened in her hair, crushing her to me. Never before had I felt like this, but then, never before had I been in love." (*"I wonder by my troth, what thou and I/ Did, till we loved?"*)

Like Eliot in *The Waste Land*, Spillane reveals exquisite awareness of modern man's flight from commitment. Hammer, rejecting both the burden of sin and the redemptive purgation that lies beyond, instead chooses the terrible freedom of life. "I . . . then put her down outside the bathroom door and mussed her hair. . . . Maybe I was a damned fool. I don't know. *I went on into the living room.*" (Author's italics.)

Although one must concede that it is not Spillane's intent to echo Donne, is that not, after all, precisely the point? Impulses springing from what Jung called the collective unconscious warrant more intensive comparative analyses of the two masters.

Millions of children and adults respond to the warmth, charm, and home-spun wisdom of the tots who populate the *Peanuts* cartoon strip. The all-suffering though resilient Charlie Brown, his nagging nemesis Lucy, and their companions including the pantophobic Linus and the philosophical beagle Snoopy, are, in effect, grown-ups with all the ideals, yearnings, frustrations, and hang-ups that adults are heir to.

One of the chief pleasures of Schultz's strip is the little comments it makes on our daily joys and troubles. Through the youngsters' amusing activities and the unvarnished directness of their conversation, we chuckle at our own foibles and idiosyncrasies.

But why let well enough alone? *The Gospel According to "Peanuts,"* a diverting but serious best seller, doesn't. With a bibliographical battery that includes theological and literary big guns such as Paul Tillich, Søren Kierke-gaard, T. S. Eliot, Karl Barth, Ernst Cassirer, Franz Kafka, and Pascal, Rob-ert L. Short, the author of the book, makes an ingenious and delightfully kitschy case of *Peanuts'* being a parable of the New Testament ethic and of Christian grace.

In elevating Snoopy to the rôle of "hound of heaven" and Lucy to an emblem of Original Sin, Short devotes as much attention to his subject as Evelyn Waugh expended in his perceptive remarks on the religious themes in Graham Greene's novels. Indeed Short, leaving no stone unturned, in the course of his book invokes Greene's *Brighton Rock*.

All of which is to say that kitsch criticism, having brought the game to bay, tends to overkill its quarry. It may be pretentious and valueless or, like the Short work on *Peanuts*, it may be entertaining and creative in its own right. In fact, *The Gospel According to "Peanuts"* both reached the top of the best-seller list and financed a doctorate in theology for Short. At least, in the realm of kitsch it is possible to serve both God and Mammon.

It is probably only an illusion, but critics seem to have made, in the name of American efficiency, a nice division of their labors. While some literary critics strive mightily to justify the most popular, innocent, and readily understood entertainment as cultural or spiritual profundities, their art critic colleagues ply their trade on the other side of the street. Because the stakes there are proportionately higher, the pitch is more strenuous.

The kitsch art criticism kit requires three indispensable elements: a painter, preferably nonrepresentational, whose tiresome repetitions of the same motifs are devoid of appeal to both a mass audience and well-informed collectors; a critic, whose disarming garrulity mingles the dazzlingly faddish with the emptily resounding; and acquisitive and highly competitive buyers who are eager to snap up the newest sensation. To the collectors, it's irrelevant if they find the paintings facile and shallow, or devoid of visual interest. For them, the real pleasure will come later, when they unload their $500 canvases on a new buyer for $125,000, thanks to the continued press agent efforts of the kitsch art critic. A tip to budding Kitsch Kritics: the following hypothetical puff seems to say everything although it says nothing.

Walter Fingal: Swatches and Blotches

The retrospective of the master of the New York School, currently at the Gallery of Modern Artists, spans nearly five years' work. In the past, not a few observers have noted that a complication in Walter Fingal's work is the puzzling dichotomy between the Swatches and the Blotches, the two major themes of his career thus far. This exhibition dispels all doubt; the Swatches represent a time of searching and the assimilation of the European tradition, while the Blotches display Fingal's achievement of a breakthrough into the avant-garde of American painting.

Between the Swatches, which date from 1971 to 1973, and the Blotches, dating from 1974 to the present time, is a subsidiary theme, the Notches. The latter interlude (1973 to 1974) represents both the culmination of the earlier period and a prefiguration of the later, and major, period. Together, they present a formidable body of work spanning nearly half a decade, and document the ineluctable development of the artist's style.

The Swatches (*Widdershins*, 1971; *Parbuckle 2*, 1973) set out Fingal's mastery of the dialectical tension between squares and circles. Leaving aside the stabbing sadness of the wedge-form Notches (*Nose Cone*, 1974), we can perceive in the Swatches haunted references to "disembodied" lines and "floating" arcs, which are, after all, the residual data of the Patches protoperiod, when the painter expressed a brief but profound interest in the mythopoeic dot.

Fingal's static Swatches have been attacked on the grounds that their emotive power depends too heavily on superficial references, as opposed to the idea or content of his more conventional contemporaries. However, the indeterminate planar regions of the superbly kinetic Blotches (*Discordia*, 1974; *Freestanding* and *Half Gainer*, 1975) tacitly declare that their colors extend beyond the limits of the canvas, blur into pulsating layers of undifferentiated aesthetic continua, and emit soft-edge luminosities that disturb the sense of equilibrium.

Ironically, the very tracing of Fingal's astonishing development, from the early naïveté of the Patches through the gathering storms of the Swatches and Notches to the apocalyptic

Blotches, misses the cumulative force of the paintings' impact. Although related austere shapes, inseparable from their colorful halations, occur with increasingly exciting regularity, it is in the enigmatic play of reductive strokes that one finds the painterly hand's most brilliant work. In them, are the felt experiences, the mystifying drama, and cryptic ambiguities that reveal, finally, Fingal's maximum effectiveness and self-acknowledged commitment to his statement.

Never underestimate the power of Kitsch!

Kitsch and the Flesh

America has taken to the murky waters of kitsch like a plastic duck to the bath. Much that is characteristic of American kitsch derives from the still strong pull of puritanism in American life, filtered through and reinforced by Victorian prudery.

Hundred-dollar-bill toilet tissue combines an embarrassed attempt to disguise bodily functions as fun with a fatuous stab at social commentary. The result is double-dyed kitsch.

Despite today's permissive mandate to let it all hang out, we see evidence of continuing Puritan and Victorian influences in America's suppressive attitude toward physiological facts of life. A coy or embarrassed reticence about bodily functions has led to a double evasion of fact, through hippopotamic humor on the one hand and pretentious prettification on the other. The honest outhouse and convenient indoor toilet have yielded to self-conscious jocosities such as Little Boys' and Girls' Rooms and toilet paper done up as hundred-dollar bills. The Powder Room, their presumably elegant counterpart, is often the most elaborately furnished unit in the house or apartment, buried beneath a jumble of fussy opulence—gilded-eagle tissue dispensers, toilet seats and tanks covered with fake tiger or zebra hide, and crystal chandeliers.

Although disguising the human body's gradual decay is hardly a new interest under the sun, in America it has become a major kitsch obsession. We have an obligation to stay young and beautiful or handsome. A profusion of sex manuals on the market tirelessly remind us that we must learn to labor harder at love-making. Jean-Paul Sartre, observing our preoccupation with presenting to the world a bouyant presence, said that in America "not to grin is a sin." Fluorescent smiles that display what Charles Lamb called, satirically, "exposed bone," real or capped; skin that owes its youthful flush to steady application of creams, ointments, washes, liners, blushes, and crushed fruits and vegetables; raised and enlarged breasts indebted to padded bras and silicone infusions; hair that's teased, tinted, and transplanted—we effect it all in a vain effort to confound the inevitable spoiler.

The kitsch culmination of the worship of youth is the attempt to annihilate death. To be sure, fear of death and awed wonder about its aftermath exist in all cultures. Even more vividly and immediately than scriptural, philosophical, and theological writings on death, the monuments man has erected to commemorate it reveal his shifting views of himself and the world.

In the course of three centuries, American stone monuments have mirrored the changing modes of mourning. In 17th-century headstones, we see how New England Puritans deprecated the perishable body with an abundance of skulls, skeletons, and grim specters holding hourglasses in one hand and scythes in the other. Although the purpose of such ornamentation was to stress the incorporeal life to come, which is the promise of Christianity, the bitter and gruesome aspects of physical death held a chilling fascination.

As life-spans lengthened and existence itself became more comfortable

for more people, funerary tastes changed. Gradually, gravestone iconography turned away from contempt for mortal life, with its severity and brutally abrupt end, to expression of sadness at its brief beauty and desirability over death. By the mid-19th century, stones emphasized death as calamity. Images of graveside mourners predominated, as draped figures stood or sat beneath drooping willows, weeping over the worst that could happen.

Today, the pretentions of kitsch all but deny the existence of death. Where once we disposed of corpses swiftly but with thoughtful ceremony, we now view Loved Ones lingeringly, applying cosmetics to enliven their appearance lest dreadful reality intrude too rudely. Burial grounds are no longer somber or lachrymose graves, but Resting Places and, in a spreading trend to ignore hard fact, Lawns.

Perhaps, after all, funerary trappings and paraphernalia, in whatever appearance, are a form of kitsch. At either extreme, we alter objective facts, either by denial of the dignity of life or by disavowal of the inevitability of at least physical extinction.

Kitsch says: It's nice to fool Mother Nature!

The All-American Kitsch Recycling Syndrome

Burdening products with the prestige of age and the sacredness of art, and a mass compulsion for forcing the utilitarian to pass to the decorative and vice versa are not exclusively American traits. Antique motifs on modern inventions—for example, plastic dinnerware with Wedgwood cameos or rococo urn cigarette lighters, both of them useful anachronisms—fill a worldwide demand.

In America, our ancestors' stern waste-not-want-not morality persists, but in debased form. For generations, frugal housewives of modest means turned colorfully imprinted cotton flour sacks into serviceable dresses, giving them another useful life. Born of necessity, that Yankee practice of using it up, wearing it out, making it do finds its modern kitsch equivalent in what can be called "conspicuous recycling."

We replace functional readaptations with a frenetic turning of everything into something else. The more jolting and eccentric the result, the more popular it is. We haunt attics, garages, secondhand stores, thrift and antiques shops in search of early coffee grinders, textile printers' rollers, and telephones to turn into lamps. We transmute blacksmiths' bellows and cobblers' benches into coffee tables, teapots and hollow flatirons into jardinières. A few years ago, a kitsch craze for using as soup tureens old and cheaply acquired chamber pots drove up their price to the point where it was less expensive, if not so fashionable, to buy real tureens.

The American current of thrift has long since disappeared in a sea of kitsch. Now, lamps are mass-produced in the shape of coffee mills, and electric clocks are set into fake wall telephones. In the realm of American kitsch, everything should seem to be something other than what it really is.

Even mundane commodities such as wastepaper baskets are designed to bear more than their utilitarian load. In fact, their often surprising form and embellishment may be sufficiently whimsical or ingenious as to become themselves the primary purpose of the article. In Great Britain and Europe, a trash receptacle is more likely to be simply that than it is in America. Suppose that in traveling abroad you have occasion to shop for such an item. Glance about any store and you're not likely to see a rubbish container, with or without a lid, in the shape of a thatched cottage or the Tower of London,

Guess that these objects are electric-light bulbs. Express amused surprise when you're told that they're not. Guess again. Give up? They're salt-and-pepper shakers (5½") in the form of objects you wouldn't expect to see on the dining table. Making useful items in the shape of other useful items is one of kitsch's favorite games.

a tumbril or the Hôtel des Invalides, a gondola or the Tower of Pisa. Of course, some of them might be produced with leather-grain embossment, rampant lions, or fleurs-de-lis. In all events, the average European accepts without misgivings a wastebasket that functions merely in terms of form.

Not so in America. Here, we expect even that lowly object to aspire to the lofty spheres of nostalgia and patriotism. "Why should I turn out just dumb wastebaskets?" we can imagine a home-accessories manufacturer asking himself. "Turn them into drums like our forefathers carried at Lexington and Concord." In their turn, millions of kitsch-oriented buyers say, "Don't give us just plastic or metal trash baskets. How about an old-fashioned milk can that'll remind me of the good old days and last summer's vacation? And put an eagle or the Liberty Bell on it so friends and neighbors will know all of us live in America."

Few of us are aware of those *multum in parvo* designs and complex consumer needs because we are inured to them. No one wonders: Is the object intended to serve principally as something useful and subordinately as decoration? Or: Is it first a charming allusion to America's past and second a rubbish can? Rhetorical questions such as those can never be answered. But by recognizing the endless and confused battle between function on the one side and form and decoration on the other, we can at least be amused by that kitsch phenomenon and find it as endlessly fascinating, and as baffling, as a Möbius strip.

Not content with ransacking the past for items to draft into present-day practical and decorative service, the American kitsch impulse is bent upon concocting an idealized past that never was, in collective historical sites where American History Comes to Life. Although "preserved villages" such as those at Sturbridge, Massachusetts, and Shelburne, Vermont, and Greenfield Village in Dearborn, Michigan, are meticulously mounted repositories of American art and artifacts, nevertheless they are synthetic creations. They

Nostalgia for America's past inspires synthetic villages such as that at Old Sturbridge, Mass. Including buildings that have been moved there from all parts of New England, and accurate to the point of absurdity, they offer a sanitized authenticity, shrouded under plastic wrap.

The brass eagle tacked on to the side of the tub is almost as much a stamp of kitsch as the fact that this "18th-century Williamsburg" ice-cream maker operates on an electric motor.

differ significantly from the restorations of already existing settlements at colonial Williamsburg, Virginia, or in Deerfield, Massachusetts, for example. To set up an artificial village, skilled antiquarians, architects, and engineers move old buildings—homes, schools, churches, smithies, general stories—from original sites across the nation and reassemble them in a tasteful, authentic arrangement.

Tourists flock eagerly to those might-have-been villages for a salutary dose of instant Americana. In the presence of impeccably packaged ghost-town nostalgia, which depends partly for its effectiveness on a sense of the past gleaned from films and historical novels, visitors experience the euphoria that Alfred North Whitehead called "vicarious vertigo."

Ultimately, the kitsch nostalgia-patriotism syndrome homogenizes everything previous to personal memory into bland "early American." Articles from the colonial and revolutionary periods collide with backbreaking Boston rockers of the mid-19th century and with turn-of-the-century kerosene lamps called—in kitschy deference to their anachronistic use in a celebrated movie—Gone With the Wind lamps.

Villages that never were, colonial Williamsburg electric ice-cream makers, bourbon bottles in the shape of the Capitol in Williamsburg—all exploit America's frenzied and indiscriminate passion for its past.

"Patriotism," said Edith Cavell, the martyred British nurse of World War I, "is not enough." Applying to random objects a stencil or decal of Old Glory draped picturesquely over an eagle-adorned drum produces neither antiques nor convincing patriotic icons. European art collections of pyxes, reliquaries, and crucifixes, like those of ancient statues of Greek and Roman deities, have won in artistic power what they have lost in religious significance. Because America is a nation still bound in the Protestant tradition, it is essentially without holy icons. Nevertheless, it seeks continuously to produce sacred objects in the form of facile patriotism. Religious articles shed their sacredness when they become décor. It's equally certain that decorative objects, however copious and well-intended their "sacred" motifs, cannot pass into the category of the divine. The attempt yields only kitsch that it useful, possibly instructive, dubiously decorative, and hardly beautiful.

When everything is something, then nothing is anything!

CHAPTER 2

Rally 'Round The Flag, Boys!

A misguided tour through politics and patriotism

Poor William Henry Harrison. No glorious deeds commemorate his administration as ninth president of the United States. He caught pneumonia at his inauguration in March 1841 and died within a month.

Even so, the credit for inventing, or at least nationalizing, the most enduring kitsch gambit in politics—the poor but honest hick—must go to the hero of the delirious "Tippecanoe and Tyler too" presidential campaign. A Virginia aristocrat from the caste that produced Washington, Jefferson, Madison, and Monroe, Harrison was the college-educated son of a wealthy plantation owner, signer of the Declaration of Independence, and governor of Virginia. In 1840, when the Whigs pitted Harrison against Martin Van Buren for the presidency, they cannily created for their gentlemanly candidate the image of a rugged frontiersman, seated before the doorway of a log cabin with a keg of hard cider beside him. His opponent was portrayed as an effete Easterner. Harrison was swept into office on a wave of campaign ribbons, parade floats, and Old Cabin Whisky—all suitably decorated with the bogus log cabin and cider jug.

Ever since then, politicians have been running on the Harrison bamboozle in one form or another. At least Lincoln depicted as a simple rail-splitter and multimillionaire Theodore Roosevelt presented as a Rough Rider had some basis in fact. On a middle ground, the gamut runs from calculated simplicity (Truman's 1948 pitch, "I work for the government and I'm trying to keep my job") to high-sounding improbabilities (Eisenhower's 1952 promise, "I will end each day thinking of millions of American homes"). But what about Nelson Rockefeller, campaigning for the New York governorship, munching a Coney Island hot dog (just like the kid next door) once every four years for the news cameras? Mrs. Nixon's "plain Republican cloth coat" was cut from the same bolt.

In recent years, the irresistible family dog has become a favorite kitsch prop. We'll never know how many votes FDR won in 1944 by defending his pet Scottish terrier against the attacks of his political enemies ("now they include my little dog, Fala"). And Lyndon Johnson never missed a chance to let his beagles lick the electoral hand that fed *him*. But it's Richard Nixon's emotion-laden and politically effective "Checkers speech" in the 1952 presidential campaign that stands as the classic of the genre. As a popular, but irrelevant, good-guy symbol, dogs have replaced the log cabin and split-rail fence, probably because they are a lot easier to come by these days.

Doublethink, the political kitsch substitute for logic, can't be claimed as an American invention. But leave it to Yankee ingenuity to improve the product. In the South, patriotism approaches the fervor of religion; antipathy to political dissenters, the heat of a crusade. Few Southerners find anything particularly ironic or incongruous in equating patriotism with the ubiquitous display of the Confederate flag, which represents the very epitome of disloyalty and rebellion. Of such is the kingdom of kitsch.

Patriotism is often the first refuge of the kitsch mind. During World War I, well-meaning muddleheads forbade the performance of works by German composers, and substituted the term liberty cabbage for sauerkraut. (That must have struck terror into the hearts of the Huns.) For twenty-five years, American philatelists were forbidden to collect stamps of the People's Republic of China. The stamps of Cuba are still banned; even picturing them in stamp catalogues is illegal. Thus, the purity of the American way of life is preserved.

Patriotic kitsch is probably the only member of the species whose silliness can, like ignorance in action, be truly dangerous and destructive. Charles Sumner, senator from Massachusetts, actually waved a bloody shirt on the floor of the United States Senate just after the Civil War. His act was instrumental in bringing about the harsh and repressive measures of Reconstruction, which caused untold hardship to the South, begetting in turn racial polarization for a century. In the late 1940s and into the 1950s, the "red" listing and consequent professional ruin of fine actors such as Mady Christians and J. Edward Bromberg, for leftist sympathies, were somehow supposed to ward off a Russian take-over of the United States during the cold war. Senator Joseph R. McCarthy's intimidation of much of the Congress and the press as he pursued an allegedly Communist army dentist through the labyrinth of Pentagon bureaucracy had all the zaniness of Harpo Marx chasing a terrified blonde. You can see the same kind of McCarthyan flag-waving hokum in patriotic activities such as the American Legion's picketing the film *Exodus* (its screenwriter was suspected of leftist leanings) or other ever-vigilant groups' seeing in the fluoridization of drinking water a brain-softening plot by Communist agents. Kitsch they all are, in its ugliest guise.

In its more innocent forms, patriotic kitsch is not enormously varied, content to use repeatedly the same emblems until they become meaningless and invisible. The American home seems to be in imminent peril of disappearing beneath a blanket of brass eagle feathers during the moulting season. Two other popular insignia are Revolutionary War drums—a favorite shape for cocktail tables and waste-paper baskets—and the stars and stripes. On canned-soup labels, sheets and pillowcases, and sneakers—how America enjoys gazing upon the flag's configurations! (Of course, manufacturers aren't averse to implying that the purchase of their stars-and-stripes-bedecked product is tantamount to casting a vote for Democracy.)

In a kind of atavistic yearning for royalty, Americans elevate movie stars into kitsch kings and queens. Lacking the saints and religious martyrs who inspire an endless supply of kitsch objects in European countries, Americans make secular saints of slain political leaders. In the past decade, John and Robert Kennedy and Dr. Martin Luther King, Jr., have become hallowed figures, joining ranks with Abraham Lincoln, who for a century held virtually solitary sway.

Military heroes come and go (or just fade away): General William T. Sherman; Admiral George Dewey, once a favored figure in bas-relief on gingerbread clocks; and General Douglas MacArthur. However, Presidents Washington, Lincoln, and Kennedy appear over and over again.

For some reason, Martha Washington is the only woman who perennially makes the best-selling kitsch list, always paired with George to make up a set of early American bookends, or in silhouette to identify the Ladies Room.

Dolly Madison, another First Lady, comes in a distant second, with little more to her name than a brand of ice cream and of kosher dill pickles.

The presidential election of 1840 marked the beginning of rip-roaring campaigns. Mass-produced dishes, banners, sheet music, and lapel ribbons transformed the patrician William Henry Harrison into a hard-drinking backwoodsman. These are two examples of Harrison's log-cabin image, and Berkeley Plantation, one of Virginia's finest Georgian mansions and Harrison's real birthplace.

"A splendid little war" is what John Hay, Ambassador to Great Britain, called the Spanish-American War in a letter to Theodore Roosevelt. Certainly for Roosevelt it was; his charge up San Juan Hill at the head of his Rough Riders provided the brand of jingoist grandstanding required for an ambitious young politician. Numerous artists romanticized that minor conflict into enduring legend. (19¾" x 13¾")

Just plain folks. Nelson Aldrich Rockefeller, in unstuffed shirt at Coney Island, performs the quadrennial Man of the People ritual expected of all candidates for governor of New York.

One demonstration of fitness to discharge the duties of president of the United States is the public kissing of babies. Here, Hubert Humphrey, the Democratic candidate in 1968, does his stuff, as Edmund Muskie, his vice presidential running mate, looks on.

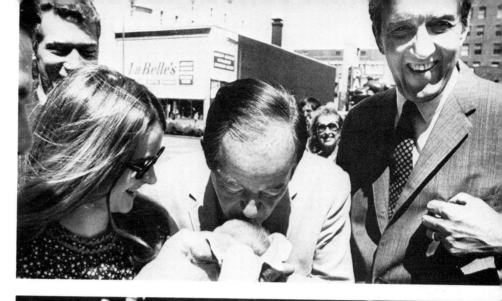

Roy Acuff, a celebrated Country and Western entertainer, uses a yo-yo in his act. President Richard Nixon, guest-appearing with Acuff at Nashville's Grand Ole Opry, on the brink of his impeachment, made a yo-man attempt at regaining popularity.

In 1928, President Calvin Coolidge, tight-lipped as ever, was inducted into the Sioux Indian tribe as Chief Leading Eagle. As meaningless political kitsch, the event was pure sitting bull.

The size of a city block (a picnic was once held on General Robert E. Lee's shoulder), it is the world's largest sculpture, and one of its kitschiest. The monstrous tableau is carved on the side of Georgia's Stone Mountain, a favorite site for Ku Klux Klan cross burnings, and commemorates the leaders of armed rebellion against the United States. In 1970, the dedication speaker was Vice President Spiro Agnew, unsparing critic of all dissenters from government policy during the Nixon administration.

"The Battle Hymn of Lt. Calley" glorifies as duty to God and Country the murder of 100 unarmed, aged, and infant Vietnamese:

> When I reach my final campground in that Land Beyond the Sun,
> And the Great Commander asks me "Did you fight or did you run?"
> I'll stand both straight and tall...And this is what I'll say:
> "Sir, I followed all my orders and I did the best I could...
> Count me only as a soldier who never left his gun..."

The record album's defense equates the atrocity with the War for Independence and the defeat of Nazism. Significantly, the album views the Confederate Stars and Bars not as an enemy flag, but as a symbol, like Lt. Calley, of dedication to patriotic duty.

Not even two American flags and an eagle can elevate this velvet and glass-bead Victorian cushion into a significant patriotic statement. (8" x 10")

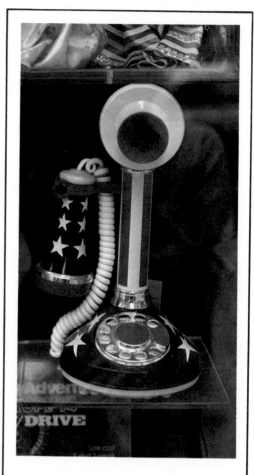

Indiscriminately using elements of the flag purely as décor, without iconographic content, robs the patriotic symbol of its power and dignity.

Cashing in on disaster to sell a product is a kitsch staple. Exploitation of patriotic fervor during the Spanish-American War is seen in this water dispenser (21") bearing a macabre decal commemorating the sunken Battleship *Maine*.

Bourbon bottles, such as this crude approximation of Andrew Jackson (12"), are dubious tributes to great men they seek to honor. That collectors pay up to $200 apiece for them demonstrates the power of kitsch.

This example of patriotic hagiolatry makes a thoughtful gift for those still mourning the passing of the late President Washington. It might even prompt a cry, like that of Shakespeare's Henry V, "God for Uncle Sam and Saint George!" The inevitable American eagle hovers above, like a holy spirit. (plate 10½")

A T-shirt design, especially as it fades, or a wastebasket ornamentation, is an ineloquent and kitsch expression of patriotic enthusiasm. In the wake of Agnew's forced resignation from the vice presidency on charges of tax evasion, the slogan "A Great American" has become still more kitschy; but the wastebasket, less so.

Immortalizing America's Bicentenary in a coffee cup, of whatever material, is routine kitsch. But these trivial plastic mugs are glorified to resemble embroidery. Simulated impossibilities, they demonstrate the muddle-headedness of kitsch. (4")

Kitsch exaggeration of the insignificant is marked by its propensity for trivializing the heroic. This brass hatrack-mirror (18" x 18") reduces to malproportioned decoration the sinking of the Battleship *Maine* and the Spanish-American War battles of Manila Bay and Santiago.

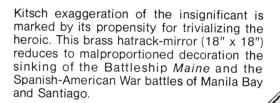

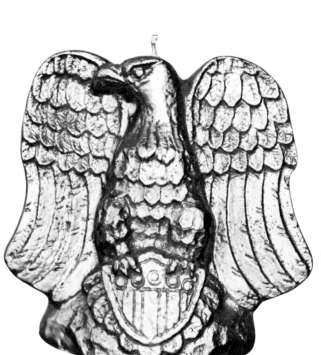

Rarely has burning patriotism found so infelicitous a manifestation as in this self-destructing national emblem. (7")

William McKinley, assassinated twenty-fifth president, offers himself as a tin snack tray (16" x 13").

JFK RFK

At first glance, this appears to be a straight-forward painting of the Kennedy brothers (16" x 11½"). Closer inspection reveals the presumptuous addition of a halo about the head of President Kennedy, suggesting sainthood.

A summit meeting of moving and talking robots rigged out to resemble Presidents Pierce, Lincoln, Andrew Johnson, Grant, Fillmore, Washington, and Jefferson suggests a time machine gone haywire. Despite the reverential aura that the inspirational speeches are supposed to induce, what really turns on the kids who visit The Hall of Presidents at Walt Disney World's Magic Kingdom, in Florida, is the supercool technology of "Audio-Animatronics."

One of kitsch's lighter moments. This hodgepodge of Revolutionary War soldier, 19th-century French hearse lantern, and automobile headlight's waffled-glass panels answers the vague yearning for a patriotic table lamp (24").

PUBLISHED BY CURRIER & IVES   Copyright 1876 by Currier & Ives, N.Y.   125 NASSAU ST. NEW YORK

CUSTER'S LAST CHARGE.

BREVET MAJOR-GENERAL GEORGE A. CUSTER, LIEUTENANT-COLONEL 7TH U.S. CAVALRY.

George Armstrong Custer (1839-76) followed up his glamorous career as the Civil War's youngest general with a spotty turn as an Indian fighter. Twice accused of abandoning his men, in 1876 the vainglorious Custer saw his chance to impress President Grant. Sent to scout the Sioux, Custer attacked their massed forces with little more than 200 men. For this suicidal caper, he was entombed at West Point, engraved by Currier & Ives, and enshrined in the hearts of a hero-worshipping nation. (10" x 13")

In 1850, Jenny Lind's **American** début at Castle Garden, in New York City, caused a sensation. Six thousand tickets were sold at auction, bringing as much as $225 each. The hysteria that followed her national tour is reflected in this "Jenny Lind" mirror (20½"). The Swedish Nightingale, in duplicate, perches precariously atop sagging branches. The American flag and shield with oak-leaf cluster perhaps salute that daring feat.

41

Oh, what lovely wars! Death in battle bestows a double blessing: it makes men heroes and wins the approbation of womenfolk. Apparently, a soldier cannot be both "dearest" and alive. This sentimentalizing of death-by-war appeared on a postcard in 1910.

The skill with which Thomas Nast (1840-1902), the father of American political cartooning, portrayed issues in black and white made him a potent force in the second half of the 19th century. When the Democratic convention of 1864 issued a call for negotiations to end the carnage of the Civil War, Nast produced this attack in *Harper's Weekly.* (The Republicans distributed over a million copies of the cartoon in that year's presidential election.) With mawkish emotionalism, Nast depicts conciliation as the abject surrender—note the inverted Union flag—of a humiliated Columbia and the mutilated North to the Confederacy's triumphantly smiling Jefferson Davis.

Uncle Sam, seated before George Washington's watchful eye, receives American doughboys, helping to make the world safe for democracy. The *Red Cross Magazine* published this painting, by Irma Deremeaux, in December 1917. Standard World War I propaganda—except for the obsequious black servant saying, in a caption, "Chrismus Gif' Massa Sam."

G. Harrold Carswell represents a near-triumph for kitsch democracy. In 1969, President Nixon nominated him to the Supreme Court, despite his lack of discernible qualifications. He received a ringing endorsement from Nebraska's Senator Roman L. Hruska: "Even if he were mediocre, there are a lot of mediocre judges and people and lawyers, and they are entitled to a little representation, aren't they? We can't have all Brandeises, Frankfurters, and Cardozos." Despite that plea, the Senate rejected the nomination.

Marcus Garvey (1887-1940) in his comic-opera uniform as self-proclaimed president-general of the wholly fictitious "African Republic," 1922. A flimflam man of epic proportions, Garvey capitalized upon the legitimate aspirations of black Americans. In 1925, he was deported to his native Jamaica for embezzling half a million dollars, which he had raised for his nationalist schemes.

The Gaudy And The Godawful

The spirit is willing but the kitsch is weak

The kitsch equivalent of religious freedom is a spiritual supermarket of self-gratification in which one takes his choice, pays his money, and goes his mystic way. The chief aim of religious kitsch is to justify the ways of man to man by making him Feel Good, all safe and snug deep down inside. Money, sex, drugs, or tearfully sentimental statuettes can help one get in touch with oneself and at the same time escape from real but humdrum problems into a fuzzy, pseudo-spiritual state. Anything is better than dreary self-discipline against the rigors of life or a stoic acceptance of one's own limitations.

Shrewd New England Puritans gave to one of the most enduring forms of American religious kitsch its original impetus. Their doctrines of salvation by faith alone and God's absolute freedom in dispensing grace meant that one could not determine by good deeds who was to be God's elect. Then how were the faithful to know that their spiritual leaders and governors (one and the same in America's sole example of theocracy) were truly chosen and thus worthy of obedience?

Among the prosperous middle class there soon evolved the notion that God would take care of His own, placing them in positions of authority and affluence. This divine sanction for prosperity became known as the Protestant Ethic. Thrift, hard work, and prudence became the preeminent Yankee virtues. Failure and poverty were the consequent signs of God's displeasure.

Kitsch, whether in art, patriotism, or religion, always fastens onto forms and externals rather than substance. By the beginning of this century, kitsch Protestantism was in high gear. Russell H. Conwell affected millions of Americans, from Wall Street to Walla Walla, with a gospel of greed that he set forth in "Acres of Diamonds," his famous sermon promising that fortunes, like happiness, are waiting to be found right in your own backyard. "I say you ought to be rich; you have no right to be poor." As good as his word, Dr. Conwell delivered his inspirational harangue more than six thousand times to paying audiences and reaped a fortune describing the joy of going into business for oneself and making money. (With part of his wealth, he founded Temple University in Philadelphia to help spread the gospel of success.) Religion was doing good for others by doing well for yourself.

No one ever better exemplified the religion of success, and the ambivalent feelings that kitsch arouses in us, than John D. Rockefeller. The power to make money, he said, was "a gift from God to be developed and used to the best of our ability for the good of mankind." The "gift" made him America's first billionaire, and the "good of mankind" he served by giving $500 million to philanthropic causes such as the University of Chicago and Rockefeller University, both of which he founded.

That business had become not only the business of America but also its religion was summed up in an anonymous businessman's prayer of the late 1920s:

God of businessmen, I thank Thee for the fellowship of red-blooded men with songs in their hearts and handclasps that are sincere; I thank Thee for telephones and telegrams that link me with home and office, no matter where I am. I thank Thee for the joy of battle in the business arena, the thrill of victory and the courage to take defeat like a good sport; I thank Thee for children, friendships, books, fishing, the game of golf, my pipe, and the open fire on a chilly evening. Amen.

Grant American kitsch religion at least one thing: its relevancy.

In 1925, religious hucksterism reached a high-water mark with *The Man Nobody Knows*, supersalesman Bruce Barton's best-selling book. Its revelation was not so much that admen and businessmen were Jesus' natural vicars (after all, it wasn't *business* that needed boosting); the good news to sing out was that He himself was a salesman at heart. Witness his copywriting technique, his adeptness at "putting [himself] in step" with his audience, and his "wonderful power to pick men."

"He would be a national advertiser today," Barton wrote, "as he was the great advertiser of his own day. Take any one of the parables, no matter which—you will find that it exemplifies all the principles on which advertising textbooks are written." The Word continues:

1. First of all they are marvelously condensed, as all good advertising must be. Jesus hated prosy dullness.
2. His language was marvelously simple—a second great essential. All the greatest things in human life are one-syllable things—love, joy, hope, home, child, wife, trust, faith, God.
3. Sincerity glistened like sunshine through every sentence he uttered. The advertisements which persuade people to act are written by men who have an abiding respect for the intelligence of their readers, and a deep sincerity regarding the merits of the goods they have to sell.
4. Finally he knew the necessity for repetition and practiced it. No important truth can be impressed upon the minds of any large number of people by being said only once.

One hand washes the other. The odor of sanctity scents the marketplace; religiosity (not necessarily the same thing as religion) blesses business. It's not surprising that *The Man Nobody Knows* has sold, to date, nearly a million copies.

Americans love a good show, and the cross-fertilization between religion and show business has enriched both of them, monetarily if not spiritually. In the early decades of this century, Chautauqua tents mushroomed every summer in thousands of cities and towns from coast to coast. Those traveling tent shows, travesties of the original center for adult education on Lake Chautauqua, New York, were a marvelous mélange of jugglers, brass bands, bagpipers, opera singers, tragedians, and religious revivalists such as Russell Conwell and fast-talking Harry "Gatling Gun" Fogleman. Even a magician was likely to be certified as a "Christian gentleman" lest yokels get the impression his uncanny powers came from the devil. The entertainment level and the cultural aims were high, bringing top-flight performers to as many as 40 million people each summer. But the religion preached was pure opportunistic kitsch, based as it was on the old show-biz axiom, "Give 'em what they want and offend nobody."

If tent-show preachers of salvation through savings accounts smacked of

P. T. Barnum, later generations of kitsch religionists have refined the formula into a lavishly produced spectacular of cynical calculation, complete with second-banana name performers, who serve as audience warmer-uppers for—at last, magic time!—the Star. From Billy Sunday and Aimee Semple ("Happy am I, I'm always happy") McPherson to Billy Graham and faith healers Oral Roberts and Kathryn ("Come and claim your cure") Kuhlman, religion as spectacle is the longest-running road show in America.

Just as show business has served as handmaiden to kitsch religiosity, religion has been a mainstay of show business. "Give me any couple of pages of the Bible and I'll give you a picture," boasted Cecil B. DeMille. For decades, the sure-fire combination of subdued orgies, dazzlingly bedecked hordes, and sin-and-retribution religion sold DeMille's blockbuster epics and their countless spin-offs. Whether parting the Red Sea, illuminating Significant Moments with mote-filled shafts of sunlight piercing gloomy thunderheads, or inflating the maudlin pieties of Lloyd C. Douglas's *The Robe* with the debut of Cinemascope, Hollywood can—or could—do it bigger and better. And with music.

For postbiblical religious profundities, the film capital relied on patriarchal clergymen who addressed everyone as "my child" or lovable good sports, such as Pat O'Brien, Barry Fitzgerald, and Bing Crosby, who brought killers to their knees or dissolved the hearts of flinty curmudgeons. All to the soaked-handkerchief delight of millions.

In the tradition of one-cent sales and cereal-box premiums, the gimmick of American religious kitsch is Give Something Extra. Although traditionally the Christian religious experience is complete in itself and often visits the witness through meditation, kitsch religion is merely a pious appendage to achieving success in worldly matters. Or just having a good time.

The same practical bent appears in kitsch religious items; for example, a two-foot-long Easter cross made of bread and studded with hard-cooked eggs. Even though the tradition is probably of European origin, the comestible cross is a welcome addition to American kitsch. It's right at home with indigenous devices such as Star of David key chains, holy-medal pocket flashlights, gummed address labels adorned with Dürer's *Hands of an Apostle*, and Saint Jude Letter openers.

Kitsch religion demands nothing from us; it expresses the ultimate in our passion for a life without inner struggle. Thanks to electronic technology, we don't have to do our own praying. We just pick up the telephone and, thanks to Dial-a-Prayer, someone somewhere will intone a petition for us on prerecorded tape. (If that fails to lift the spirit, there's Dial-a-Joke.)

Even more than the materialists whom they profess to despise, followers of ever-new fads and sensations—astrology, scientology, aesthetic realism, UFOs, drugs at home or at Woodstock, gurus, transcendental realism—have as their goal easy answers and guaranteed rewards. The fact that all these escapist kitsch diversions are peddled by external agencies rather than acquired by personal perceptions seems to matter not at all to the herd instincts of the mass hysteric.

That these evasions are seen by many observers as a rebirth of religion in our own day is the ultimate triumph of kitsch.

Norman Vincent Peale's *The Power of Positive Thinking* is a multimillion-copy pep talk that promotes faith as good business. The Reverend Mr. Peale tells the story of the man who, wanting to bring Jesus' "mustard seeds of faith" to others, encased real seeds in plastic to be used as key-chain fobs, and made a fortune selling them. Peale's inspirational best seller is available on Bible paper, suitably gilt-edged.

Spending as much as a million dollars to promote and stage one of his crusades, Billy Graham was once named Salesman of the Year by the New York Sales Executive Club. "I am selling the greatest product in the world," he said. "Why shouldn't it be promoted as well as soap?" His razzle-dazzle variety shows have been seen by more people than the population of the world at the time of Jesus. The unofficial White House chaplain in the Nixon administration proudly points out, "Saint Paul didn't have television."

Aimee Semple McPherson (1890-1944) was variously called the Barnum or the Mary Pickford of religion and "the titian-haired whoopee revivalist." Her international fame as founder of the Foursquare Gospel rested as much on her headline-making show-biz savvy (a kidnapping hoax, rose-scented baptismal water, a series of sensational lawsuits) as on her promise of paradise. The Happiness Girl's spine-tingling, satin-gowned entrance down a runway from the balcony "heavens" of her Angelus Temple, in Los Angeles, never failed to send her throng of followers into a spiritual transport.

Oral Roberts is a miracle man in the Elmer Gantry tradition. Through the wizardry of television, his cures—between the commercials—are equally successful for shut-ins, who have only to gaze at the screen at home to be restored to health.

Cecil B. DeMille chose Charlton Heston to play ▶ Moses in *The Ten Commandments* (1956) because of the brawny actor's resemblance to Michelangelo's statue of the law-giver. But in marcelled wig and beard, atop a canvas-and-plaster Mount Sinai, Heston came closer to being a Sunday-school coloring book caricature.

Biblical blockbusters differ from Westerns, not in their depth of moral vision, but by portraying chiefly the good guys as glum and wearing the drab clothes. The real gusto is expended on scenes of pagan wickedness, generally featuring belly dancers and loin-clothed musclemen. *The Prodigal* (1955) permits a sleekly dressed Lana Turner, as high priestess to Baal, to preside over a temple remarkably like a movie-palace lobby. In the Golden Calf sequence of *The Ten Commandments,* an idolatrous Edward G. Robinson has tied hapless Debra Paget to Bibleland's equivalent of the railroad tracks. In the next episode of this kitschy melodrama, Charlton Heston foils the villain.

Ben-Hur (1959) did best what Hollywood has always done best, from the Keystone Kops to *The French Connection*—the thrilling chariot race. Consistent with its obsession with human interest and its kitsch notion of Higher Purpose, Jesus' crucifixion serves to bring boy and girl together at the fadeout and to cure the hero's mother and sister of what is supposed to be leprosy but appears to be only stubborn cases of acne.

A scene from Nazimova's kitsch-classic film, *Salome* (1922). Turning Aubrey Beardsley's art nouveau illustrations for Oscar Wilde's hothouse play into real sets and costumes made them merely hilarious. Here, a Biblical Peter Pan demands delivery of John the Baptist's head.

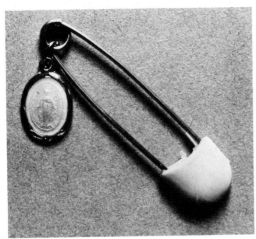

It's best to leave some things secular. The diaper pin (2″), available in baby pink or blue, dangles a Virgin Mary holy medal. Failure to foresee inevitable drenching has resulted in kitschy-coo.

The ideal letter opener for monthly bills. Not even the fact that Saint Jude wrote a New Testament epistle imparts appropriateness to this piece of molded plastic (6½″).

The manufacturers of these chocolates see nothing amiss in turning sacred symbols of God's deliverance of Israel from Egyptian bondage into after-dinner goodies. But they boggle at reproducing the Star of David on the foil wrappers, and so represent it incomplete. Call this double-think kitsch.

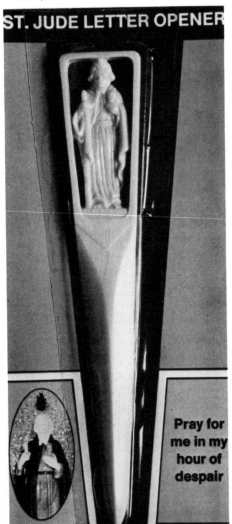

ST. JUDE LETTER OPENER

Pray for me in my hour of despair

More Transylvania than transfiguration, this "enhancement" of Dürer's drawing *Hands of an Apostle*, rendered in a pallid flesh-like plastic (7″), suggests leftovers from Dr. Frankenstein's laboratory. As they turn about to the tune of "Bless This House," the effect is decidedly not spiritual.

Man does not live by bread alone, but by selling these kitschy "Graceline" napkins to those who "appreciate the simplicity of gracious table prayers as symbols of reverence and thanksgiving." Unlikely to arouse a deeper response than a passing "Oh, how lovely," they are an example of disposable kitsch piety.

More disembodied hands (8" each). Why a pen holder should express reverence is unclear. A night lamp of glowing hands that lights the way to the bathroom is disquieting rather than comforting.

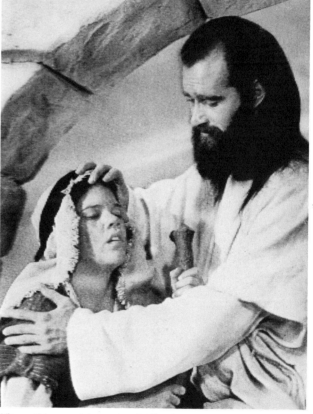

Wind up this doll-faced Madonna and Child (7½") and watch them revolve while the harem-like cushion tinkles Schubert's "Ave Maria."

When this card is moved, the blind boy's eyes open, an on-the-spot miracle thanks to three-dimensional photography. Also available at the local drugstore is a head of the crucified Jesus, with 3-D drops of blood and fluttering eyelids. Godhead reduced to technological gimmickry has more to do with selling postcards than with spreading the Word.

The bigger the better. Amid ads for hair cream, soda pop, and pain-relievers, the Bible competes mightily at a Jehovah's Witnesses convention in New York's Yankee Stadium.

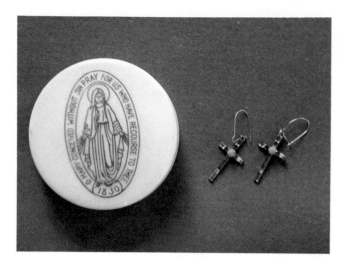

Eros and *caritas* collide in both this pink plastic, Hail Mary face-powder box (2½") and the enticing intent of earrings (1") in the form of the most sacred emblem of Christianity.

◄ Flashy poverty and hypnotic chanting by throngs of people characterize the new youth-movement religions. Providing a more sustained emotional massage than drugs or rock festivals, they are similarly devoted to "heightened consciousness" or feeling good. At left, thousands of Jesus People jam the Cotton Bowl in Dallas, Texas, at Expo '72. Below, Krishna Consciousness purification immerses 5,000 adherents in an emotional bath at the Rathayatra Car Festival in San Francisco's Golden Gate Park, in 1970.

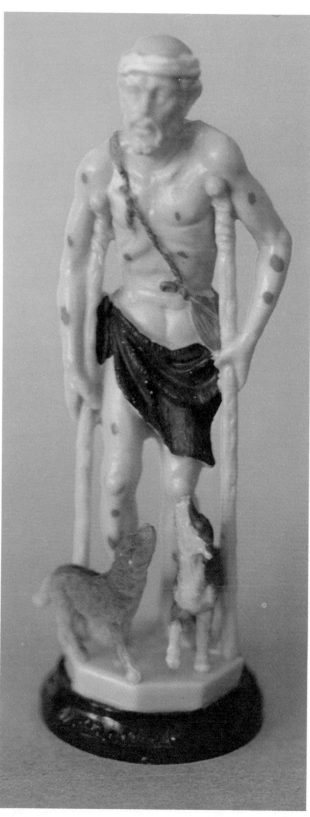

This Lazarus (4"), dogs licking his gruesomely realistic sores, is for mounting on the dashboard, next to the sunglasses, change holder, and cigarettes. In the casual context, something of its religious force is lost.

An ill-conceived try at packing religiosity into candles (7"). Praying hands or Jesus' head melting before one's eyes is, at the very least, horror-movie kitsch.

The crass juxtaposition of streamers of ten- and twenty-dollar bills with the reliquary of a saint who died for other-worldly values makes the annual Festival of Saint Gennaro in New York a kitsch *stravaganza.*

Charming snowscape paperweights are travestied in this incongruous religious object (3½"x4"). A flashing red light, like those used as highway accident signals, illuminates the plastic bauble. Inside, gold "snow" swirls about the solemn scene on Calvary.

Wearing red sackcloth and wooden yokes around the neck, and playing Battle of Armageddon, provide in-the-thick-of-it drama for bored middle-class youths. The impending appearance on January 31, 1974, of the comet Kohoutek revealed to the Children of God that the Day of Judgment was at hand for a wicked America. Neither the alleged divine revelation nor the heralded celestial spectacle came off as scheduled.

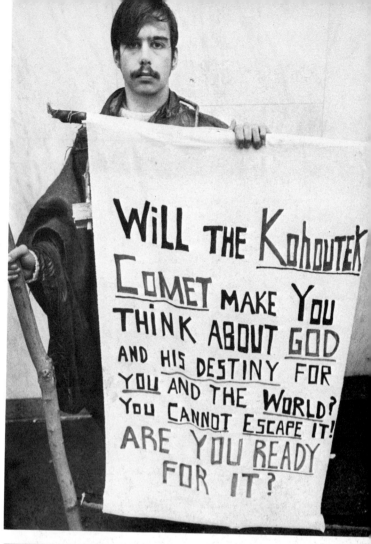

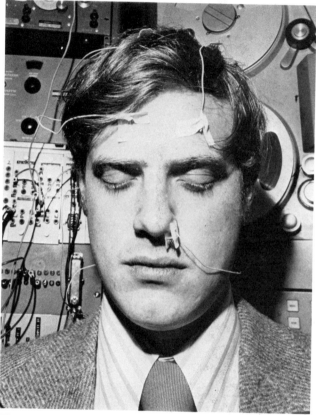

That new-time religion—if it's good enough for the Beatles, it's good enough for me. Transcendental Meditation is one of many narcissistic self-awareness cults that grew up in the uncertain sixties. Here, one of the faithful gets in touch with his feelings.

Maharaj Ji, a teen-age guru, has parlayed mystical moonshine and humility into a personal fleet of sports cars, Rolls-Royces, and a $22,000 British Jensen touring car for festivals.

57

The American staging of the British rock opera *Jesus Christ Superstar* made the Passion an excuse for a simplistic Vietnam War protest. The combination of trendy nudity, flower children, and over-production made the play relevant kitsch. Here, in the American movie version (1973), hardhats crucify the hippie Messiah.

Knock, knock. Who's there? This widely available reproduction of an oil painting (16"x21") reduces the rôle of God in the affairs of men and nations to that of a droopy, sentimental Jesus begging entrance to the United Nations. The vapidity of the figure, contrasting strikingly with its bizarre proportions (which conveniently match the size of the building), weakens rather than strengthens the wispy concept.

THIS PUZZLE IS SOLVED BY FINDING THE RIGHT BIBLE VERSES WHICH FIT IN, AND WHEN COMPLETED, THE ENTIRE PUZZLE IS A <u>READABLE STORY</u> OF THIS SUBJECT.

Jesus said, "I am with you alway." He may have been anticipating Bible-Graphics' crossword puzzle, framed in simulated walnut cardboard, suitable for hanging (16"x12").

The doctrine that God approves of those engaged in a "just war" is reduced to triviality. Imitating soldiers before a battle, a football team prays for victory over the wicked enemy. (Guess what the other team is doing.)

This cardboard wall plaque (9"x11") does its kitschy best to extract humor from the Twenty-third Psalm. Such desecration of the sacred disguised as cleverness produces a thrill of naughtiness.

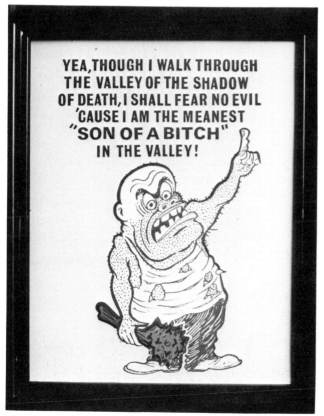

YEA, THOUGH I WALK THROUGH THE VALLEY OF THE SHADOW OF DEATH, I SHALL FEAR NO EVIL 'CAUSE I AM THE MEANEST "SON OF A BITCH" IN THE VALLEY!

Religion covers—or uncovers—a multitude...Communicants at the Hi-Life Social Club Church in Pasadena, Calif., salute the topless-bottomless celebrant. America's freedom of religion from regulation or legal prosecution spawns exceedingly bizarre forms of worship.

59

CHAPTER 4

Everything But The Kitschen Sink

Household hints from *Home Desecration*

Dear Edie and Fred,

Three cheers for your cheery house! We've both been talking about nothing else but your housewarming ever since we got back home. A good name for your remodeled triumph would be Miracle on Grover Avenue, but the sign on the lawn is exactly right--The Edens' Garden. Who says you can't create your own paradise?

At first, we thought you had a real zoo in front of your home. The couple we came with pointed out that the duck family and the deer and the flamingo were actually plastic. Naturally; but for a moment we were really amazed, which is the whole idea.

The entrance hall is truly impressive. How many homes have simulated <u>crystal</u> chandeliers? The thriving cactuses in the huge old-timey Chinese vases and the grotto sporting the fountain with the babe in the buff pouring water into an illuminated scallop shell set an elegant tone for the entire house.

Your family room, accessorized with fabulous Americana touches--from the blue denim tieback draperies to the red-and-white checkerboard no-wax flooring and sky-blue ceiling with fluffy white cloud stencilling--is a knockout. What a great idea for a sofa--covering an old church pew in Early American patchwork fabric. A room wrapped up in photo murals of Yellowstone National Park, Independence Hall, New England meadows and mountains, and San Francisco Bay shows a professional touch indeed. And to think they're all washable! The vivid colors made us feel we were actually standing in all those places at the same time. Which one of you clever Edens thought of a ship's-wheel ceiling fixture with the flame bulbs in traditional Mason jars? (A confession: we're electrifying an old wagon wheel to play up the rustic look in our French Provincial family room, but we're using small pleated silk shades over the lights for a more formal effect.) What impressed us most in that room was the knotty-pine Early American entertainment center--a fireplace unit with electric logs, TV, stereo, record storage, books, and a bar. Perhaps most striking of all was the butcher-block table, perfect for displaying Fred's collection of Nazi souvenirs.

We're going to steal another idea right off your Mediterranean living-dining room floor. That indoor-outdoor simulated flagstone rug made us believe in magic carpets all over again. We could hardly tell the redwood paneling was contact paper. Over the traditional Conquistador sectional

sofa, the pair of matador paintings have the look, feel, and
thrill that only original, signed oils can have. On the
opposite wall, Van Gogh's Sunflowers, done in buttercup and
goldenrod yarns, is a radiantly warm masterpiece. By the
way, you must tip us off to where you got your new refectory
table. It looks actually old.

The fake-zebra stair runner prepared us for the creative
genius you've lavished on the floor above. We can't decide
which is more exciting, the country casual bath or your
country chic bedroom. . . .

And so on, until "Happy house, Betty and Bob." One can either play What's
Amiss in This Picture? or complete the letter from personal observation.

In a kitsch house (or apartment) that is intended to awe both its occupants
and visitors with a multiplicity of strained effects and at the same time provide homelike comfort, there need be only a few strokes that are authentic
kitsch. For example, "Fred Eden's" Nazi curio collection doesn't by itself
qualify as kitsch, unless it includes a swastika-decorated carving set. However, it does so if the objects are exhibited infelicitously on a butcher-block
table, suggesting not only the slaughtering of animals but also, by virtue of
the items on display, the carnage of millions of noncombatant human beings in concentration camps. In any case, such mementos of World War II
are painfully unsuitable in a room dedicated to carefree recreation. Real or
imitation flagstone carpeting might be fitting as porch or patio flooring,
but even the presence of genuine flagstone in a formal interior room is difficult to explain. Simulation of the unlikely is kitsch par excellence. There's
no compelling reason why one can't press into service a Mason jar (named
for John L. Mason, an 18th-century American inventor) for use other than
home canning. But an imposed alliance between objects suggesting domestic
frugality and maritime outfittings results in a clash of disparate elements,
a hallmark of kitsch. Vincent van Gogh's Sunflowers is an undoubted masterpiece; yet a reproduction done in yarn is a decorative simulacrum having
only general reference to the colors and configuration of the original painting.

The Edens hoped to create an imposing house, a giant but tasteful conversation piece. However, the hyped-up decorating advice that fills "bright idea"
magazines and newspaper columns has led them down the garden path of
kitsch. Whenever possible, those guides imply, everything should resemble
something other than what it is, and every room must have an immediately
recognizable theme or twist—Early American recreation rooms, sunken living rooms, elevated dining rooms, either glamorous or archly rustic bathrooms, kitchens with the Texas Look, the California Look, or the Persian
Look.

In the kitschography of such endeavors, "personalized decoration" means
stuffing rooms with the mass-produced furniture and embellishments advertised heavily in home-improvement guides for sale at newsstands and
supermarket check-out counters. Terms such as "Renaissance," "Colonial
Spanish," or "Italian" cover any piece of period-style furniture stained dark
walnut and abundantly oiled. The addition of "wormhole" drillings, often
called "distress marks," produce an even more convincing antique effect.
"Authentic Early American" means generally any light wood slathered in
carrot-colored varnish masquerading as maple, although our ancestors
painted light woods—including maple—black, dark green, or blue, except
for an occasional kitchen worktable, which they left plain.

Lament the leveled forests that provide unsightly knot-marred lumber for Early American wall "paneling." In early houses, wood paneling was always true paneling; that is, harmonious arrangements of raised and recessed sections. Southern houses were likely to have walls of richly glowing walnut. Elsewhere, walls and dadoes, like the furniture, were always painted in colors such as off-white, medium blue, or tan. Even under the paint, there was only the finest, knot-free pine. However, our forebears did use knotty pine in abundance—for firewood.

Knotty-pine wallpaper, favored by those who demand the cachet of authentic early American atmosphere, without its expense, is kitsch raised to the third power—the imitation of an imitation of the nonexistent. But rooms containing "coordinated" decorative touches such as Early American electronic entertainment centers, Liberty Bell coaster sets, and paper or plastic "wood" wall coverings comprise, after all, what the kitsch-decoration magazines like to call a "theme."

Kitsch décor betrays itself also in its attempt to have it both ways. For example, should we settle for an ordinary sofa covered in a durable, but attractive, cloth, or risk the expensive splendor of delicate brocade? Kitsch offers a no-risk solution. We can have the best of both worlds by choosing the more impressive fabric for a casually extravagant air that indicates our better-than-average taste. Then, we may embalm the sofa in a clear plastic slipcover. The catch is that we won't sit on and delight in the comfort and beauty of luxurious brocade; instead, we'll sit on plastic. Though we may gaze through the protective shield to the elegance beneath, the sofa may as well have been upholstered in a dollar-smart fabric for all the low-yield hedonism to be derived from furniture-in-a-baggie.

Similarly, if we value ever-flourishing plastic plants and flowers, and bowls of tempting wax or plastic fruit over their perishable counterparts, we prefer resemblance to reality. Such preference marks the ultimate alienation from an interested, even concerned, rapport with our surroundings. Like the Edens' matador paintings, the counterfeits are mere props in a stage-setting house that relegates even its owners to the status of visitors who have no personal commitment to what they admire. In addition, we become like our furnishings, eclectic and ambiguous creatures, dependent on our fantasy-Mediterranean rooms to endow us with a cosmopolitan identity.

"Take our word for it, baby. You're doing your own thing your own way when you do our thing our way," purr the "designers' portfolio" kitsch guides. By adopting their taste for ours, we never know what our own is. The pretentious entrance hall, mishmash of an Early American family room, country casual bathroom, and country chic bedroom signal the Edens' snobbish notion of opulence, their naively expressed enthusiasm for America, and their down-to-earth folksiness, with a touch of urban sophistication. Where is the room that they planned and decorated for themselves, not their friends, before other rooms created façades for them? For those whose individuality comes in kitsch kits and caboodles, the question doesn't exist.

This **well house, on the lawn of a house in suburban** New York, **has** neither a rope to raise and lower the bucket nor a **well** beneath it. The three-foot-high mirage is, like the forlorn wagon wheel, dead-end kitsch.

A peaceable kitsch kingdom. The flowers, including those "planted" in the good, fertile earth, are plastic.

Genuine crystal prisms make musical sounds when they move; glitter, when they catch the light. These rigid blobs of dull plastic (12½") catch only dust.

Not a drunk's nightmare, but a bootlegger's dream house. Garish grandeur was the passion of George Remus, the most flamboyant of Prohibition liquor merchants. A clutter of elephants and classical pillars, and a jungle of vines and flowers crowd the entrance of his castle in Cincinnati, Ohio. By comparison, the Italian marble swimming pool is a model of restraint, but the kitsch itch to overdo finds full expression in the endless greenery.

Faithful reproductions of furniture styles from other countries are compliments to their fine craftsmanship. But this exploitative Instant Congo set affronts the beautiful designs indigenous to Africa. Such kitsch patronizes both the unwary buyer of the pieces and the culture of their implied origin. Note particularly the anomalous "primitive" coffee table.

Kitsch has been called the only art form developed by the middle class. But the pretentious mishmash of styles in William H. Vanderbilt's mid-19th-century New York drawing room makes it a blue-blood kitsch Mecca—and Rome—and proto-Hollywood.

One of the jewels in the diadem of the Madonna Inn, San Luis Obispo, Calif., embodies to perfection the arbitrary joining of disparate elements that marks High Kitsch. The room resembles a set for a tank-town production of *The Marriage of Figaro* held in a barn. In the topsy-turvy world of kitsch, wood is for walls (modern, rustic, or early anything), never for floors. The wing chairs covered in blue plastic enhance the some-of-this some-of-that atmosphere.

The "Bridal Falls Suite," which unhappily resembles a furnished crypt, boasts a waterfall shower as "a unique conversation piece." The heavy-handed extravagance of this décor makes it Supreme Kitsch.

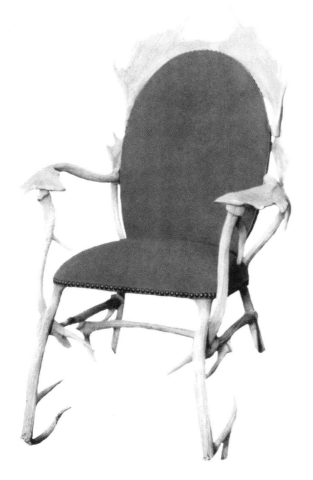

Not a tacky, grotesque chair fashioned of antlers, but an aluminum replica "carefully antiqued by hand to resemble the mellow, weathered aspect of true horn." The seat cover is "taupe pigskin vinyl." Ecological kitsch does not come cheap; the chair costs $425.

Pretentious boutiques sell portable liquor cabinets coyly disguised as a grouping of leather-bound books. They offer also cigarette boxes behind the same mask. Here is the most pointless dissemblance of all: a bookshelf filled with a fantastic instant home library to make it look like—a bookshelf.

Here stands an all-plastic Early American tall-case clock, scooped out to house a bookcase (5'6"). Its hollow pretense at a combination that never was is further emphasized by the artificial books and ferns.

A spread of eagles serves this gas-log fireplace. The demilune hearth rug (40"x21½") is of fireproof black canvas; the eagle and stars, in gold paint, lend "a decorator's touch of elegance." The milk can masquerading as a kindling-wood container (19") is in reality a piece of plastic pretending to be a milk can masquerading as . . .

For anyone not lucky enough to own a real gas-log imitation fireplace, there are fake ones in imitation stone, in imitation brick, or in sheet metal, with inflammable decorative spindles. (And an eagle.) Even the "fire" is imitation—it's electric.

The permutations of kitsch are countless. *Left:* Nothing more than a note pad, the plaster-of-paris frame in high relief represents every cliché of an Early American kitchen hearth. The pencil cleverly doubles as the churn's agitator. (7") *Right:* The fireplace lamp base groans under the burden of a globe that, if proportion were observed, would be the size of a small ascension balloon. This preposterous kerosene lamp struggles for tradition, but must settle for kitsch. (8")

From bean pot to toilet seat, from embroidery-covered brick doorstop to matching apron and pot-holder set, the full-fledged kitsch house is an aerie of painted, cast, etched, and gilded eagles.

Next only to eagles, wrought iron and philodendron (real and plastic) appear to form the twin pillars of kitsch décor. Nothing is more natural to those oblivious to incongruity than combining the two in this miniature water pump (8½") and senselessly lugging it into the house.

Cheap pottery that simulates fine German Meissen china is standard schlock. But it is kitsch's confused vision that merges this planter into a flatiron (6"). This knickknack merits two of kitsch's highest accolades, "clever" and "adorable."

Kitsch's unwillingness to leave bad enough alone produced this iron-skillet ashtray (3") with a Puritan maid's face to stub out cigarettes on.

The light that never was, on sea or land—except in the fantasy realm of kitsch. Nothing, except the perverse appeal of kitsch, recommends this alliance between a Donald Duck-like ocean fish, fresh-water naiads, and the land-locked lamp itself (12½"x14").

This replica of a turn-of-the-century French telephone has been modernized by the addition of a functional dial system. But it has been also kitsched up by the addition of a muddy reproduction of an 18th-century scene crowded onto the dial.

The jollying up of physiological facts is a favorite concern of kitsch. This comical false-teeth holder (4") comes personalized with the owner's name. When the cover is lifted, a music box cutely plays "The Shadow of Your Smile."

71

Rear: Perched precariously between dignity and demeaning décor, this debased bronze-like American eagle is pinioned to a simulated-walnut toilet seat. *Foreground, left:* Sir Winston Churchill (a brandy fancier) delivers his historic "Iron Curtain" speech at Fulton, Missouri, from a 100-proof bourbon bottle. *Right:* From marble majesty to paltry plastic—a faint echo of a caryatid from the Acropolis' "Porch of the Girls" becomes a bubble-bath dispenser.

Ingenuity created the knife sharpener-can opener combination. Kitsch inspired this radio and tissue roller (6½"x9"). Ebenezer Scrooge would have smiled in vindication at the humbug holiday cheer of Santa Claus toilet paper.

America's bathrooms play dress-up as Spanish haciendas and as Turkish seraglios. So why not as Tarzan and Jane's tree house? Bathrooms are notably subjected to the kitsch impulse to Go Creative.

In this store-window display, the liquor and hi-fi cabinet, flanked by what-nots with hanging lamps, awaits only the lighting of the electric logs to radiate its icy charm. The manufacturer has lavished every symbol of *Godfather* elegance on this plywood altar to Status.

From barn to bar stool. This dairy-farm milk can (24") is no more comfortable for being stenciled with hex signs and a Currier and Ives winter scene. Kitsch is more concerned with ingenuity than with function.

Blatant appeal to Mexican-Americans is evident in this bogus "Aztec" living-room ensemble. The vague evocation of pre-Columbian motifs combined with Victorian bordello crushed red velvet and tasseled tie-back draperies produces an all-purpose paean to no-purpose kitsch.

Emerging from the limbo of kitsch, this figurine (6") raises a perplexing problem. From the neck down, the nurse appears to be a child; the head, in structure, hairdo, and makeup, is that of a woman. What, then, is the object in her arms—a large doll or an undersized baby? Label this pottery gewgaw Unregistered Nurse.

Credit Walter Keene, America's favorite kitsch painter of bug-eyed kids, with inspiring these figures (7"). Such saccharine portrayal of children exploits the hankering after dream children of an earlier age.

Which is more American—the ice-cream cone or the Statue of Liberty? This pop-art night light (8½") resolves the problem by embodying the two in a single object that demeans the dignity of the monumental hand bearing the torch of freedom, and at the same time elevates the significance of frozen custard to the status of Liberty.

Attempting to make this realistic couple arty by Giacometti-like elongation results only in repulsive, pinheaded kitsch. (8½")

CHAPTER 5

The Old Sell Game

This just has to be the most fabulous (foolish),
fantastic (flagrant), far-out (fatuous)...

Even if we could live by bread alone, bakers would scramble for our trade.
In 1974, American advertisers spent $26 billion bombarding their country-
men with compelling reasons why this brand or that service outranks its
competitors.

Essentially, advertisers put us on notice that should we fail to buy or pa-
tronize their wares we risk the Unfulfilled Life for ourselves and our families.

New Antiques

You don't have to shop in out-of-the-way places to
find "antiques" like these! Fesco has recreated these
smart Early American collector's items in durable, modern
plastics. And, they're available at prices even grandma
would have thought reasonable!

The unique coal scuttle in colonial red or black holds
fireplace logs, magazines or newspapers.
Lift the upper half of the "little brown
jug" and you have a wastebasket,
planter or a handy place to keep yarns
and needles. The milk can and barrel
can be a wastebasket, a floral container
or an umbrella stand. Or, go creative.

Want to collect antiques the easy way? These oxymoronically labeled "new antiques" are really just as good as old things, except to those with nothing better to do than frequent "out-of-
the-way places." This ad is unusually kitschy because the original items, so lovingly reproduced, are neither antique, nor early American, nor were they fancied up with eagles. All of them
were mass-produced utensils available in hardware stores up to the 1940s, at least.

Frantic pursuit of the sensational attention-getter is typical of kitsch advertising. Humanoid worms are even more repellent when consorting with crawling real worms, gnawing away at the mulberry leaf.

Man's mythic struggle to free himself from abject dependence on the jealous gods finds a powerful statement in the legend of Prometheus. That primal benefactor of the race stole fire from heaven and gave it to mankind. As punishment for his defiance, Zeus chained him to a mountain, where an eagle plucked continually at his liver. Maxfield Parrish, in this mildly kitschy poster of 1919, implied that the young Titan suffered the wrath of Zeus so that General Electric might sell light bulbs.

This statuette of the 1930s is meant to sell women's shoes. However, the parted gown of the autovoyeuristic woman and the mirror transform the figure into near-pornography. The reflected view is unobstructed all the way to her unclothed torso. The effect is one of fetishism and exhibitionism. (21")

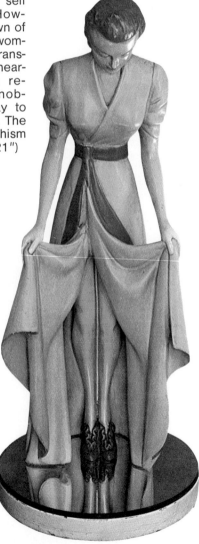

Washday drudgery made sexy. In this early example of an abiding theme in American advertising, a carefree lass cavorts provocatively on the phallic "wiggle" stick.

Kitsch advertising, glorifying the superficial and magnifying the trivial, plays cynically on our anxieties—real or imagined—and exploits them tactlessly, tastelessly, even ruthlessly. Instead of emphasizing the functional or qualitative superiority of their products, advertisers endow them with near-magical properties that guarantee romantic conquest ("Often a Bridesmaid But Never a Bride") and business and social success ("How to Win Friends and Influence People").

A century or so ago, among the ads for bustles and bowlers, shirtwaists and starches, our great-grandparents came upon patent-medicine panaceas for Tragic Ailments such as impotence, "female troubles," alcoholism, and venereal diseases. In succeeding decades, business and its hired drumbeaters developed fresh fields of human fears. No longer victims of shameful maladies only, we found ourselves wanting in more serious ways. To our horror, we discovered that personal failings bedeviled our chances of success. We should be basking in the esteem of our betters (those who ought to comprise our social circle) and forging ahead at the office. Instead, the ads revealed, we were all dwelling miserably and needlessly in Nowhereville, powerless to be born into refined society or to ascend the brightest heaven of executive leadership.

Luckily, hundreds of mail-order establishments were at hand to remedy our pitiful lacks. Pleading guilty to the implied accusation of the Sherwin Cody School of English ("Do You Make These Mistakes in English?"), we willingly sentenced ourselves to a correspondence course that would rehabilitate us for social acceptance. If we took up the U.S. School of Music's offer of a "few months" of mail-order instruction, no longer would laughing friends deride when we sat down at the piano and started to play *Liebestraum* or the *Moonlight* Sonata. Purification of a literary nature could enter our homes on a monthly basis ("without waste or worry") if we joined book clubs, whose wise graybeards would show us the way and the life through Worthwhile Reading. If those sedentary pursuits of self-improvement caused ambitious but puny lads to neglect their physical development, the Charles Atlas course would turn them into muscular marvels, ready to prove themselves Real Men by countering insults with knockout blows to their tormentors' jaws.

At the flinty heart of most advertising-through-ridicule is the desire to instill in us a gnawing fear that we're basically contemptible, or at least laughable, and ill-equipped to take our place among those whom we admire or envy. Long before Amy Vanderbilt became the *doyenne* of social certitude, two other vastly popular captains of comportment pledged themselves to steer us away from the reefs and shoals of socially fatal blunders into the snug harbor of proper behavior. Emily Post's *Etiquette: The Blue Book of Social Usage* (the more durable guide, having gone into nearly a hundred printings) was a volume of practical advice ("Corn on the cob, eating of"; "Fish, removing bones from"; "Nuts, at dinner or lunch") that charmed by a *dramatis personae* reminiscent of characters in a Restoration play— the Toploftys, the Smartlingtons, the Kindhearts, the Worldlys, the Oldnames. In advising a socially insecure middle-class America, Miss Post stressed the simple verities of tact and kindness as the basis of all good manners.

By contrast, the two-decker *Book of Etiquette* ("A Social Secretary for Life"), by Lillian Eichler, an ad copywriter turned dictator of decorum, was a kitsch compendium of waking nightmares portraying ordinary people as utter boobs, perpetually disgracing themselves by their inadequacy in the face of every social contingency. "Has This Ever Happened to You?" (and of course it had) Miss Eichler sneered in the illustrated ads she wrote for her book. Each display depicted a social gaffe or impasse ("Do you know how to write a letter to a titled person?"). In one ad, a young woman, visibly haunted by her lack of French, sits paralyzed before a menu. As she's done on date after date, she plays it safe: "A chicken salad, please." In another, a well-dressed couple, clearly beyond their depth in a fine restaurant, fumble helplessly before an elaborate table setting, while a waiter smirks at their want of savoir-faire. After embarking on their meal, Miss Eichler's ad copy tells us, the couple are incapable of conversing in a "calm well-bred manner." The palsying perils of dining out were only a few of the problems that could be solved by returning the coupon, with $1.98, and awaiting the arrival of a plain carton.

Kitsch advertising wants to say something important, yet it forever reduces its message to a level of intellectual triviality. It thrives simplistically on the assumption that, like broken wind-up dolls, we do nothing right and from sheer perverseness invariably own the wrong brand of everything. When we allow ourselves to be nagged and badgered into buying the "right" product, our reward is rarely our personal satisfaction; rather, we do it to impress other people and endow ourselves with an all-new—always improved—personality.

If we use a detergent that takes our dirty laundry all the way from white to bright, marveling neighbors, clamorous in their envy, will crowd around our dazzling clothesline. The right car is not only comfortable and economical to run, but also bestows on us an irrefutable image of success. Our failing powers, blasphemous over-thirty obsolescence, and inability to cope with present and future shock all disappear with the "Drink Me" blandishments of soft-drink advertising that assure us a place in the wonderland of the Pepsi Generation.

By exploiting our deep-seated fears of inferiority, kitsch advertising transforms us into its own image of all that is desirable: supersexed, the center of attention, the envy of our peers. As we move, instantly and effortlessly, from triumph to triumph through our acquisition of more and more products, kitsch advertising always sees us, like Satan, about to be flung from the ramparts if we fail to Keep Up. To that extent, at least, we're like the women in certain television commercials whose otherwise exemplary lives fall apart if they omit Clorox from their washday ritual. As the White Queen might have remarked to Alice: "The rule is, contentment tomorrow and contentment yesterday—but never contentment *today*."

All our grace, all our sentiments, all our ideas come to exist not in ourselves but in the objects we buy—our patriotism in the flag we wear in our lapels, our parental love in the brand of paper diaper in which we swaddle our babies, our status in the Bigelow carpet on the office floor, our self-respect in mouthwash, underarm deodorant, feminine-hygiene spray.

From the macho-fantasy of a male-populated Marlboro Country to a greeting card that shows (read: *proves*) we cared enough to send the very best, countless advertising slogans wear one or another of the guises of kitsch. But few ads embody all of the characteristics in one grand grotesquerie. One that did plumb that nadir appeared some years ago in popular national magazines. It pictured an elderly woman peering apprehensively through a window into the pelting rain outside as she worries about the possibly inadequate casket in which her late husband lies buried. "Is seepage," the ad's headline intoned bathetically, "disturbing your loved one?"

Even if we cease to tremble with fear that we're failing our family, washing its clothes ineffectively, offending it with body effluvia, becoming a grouch because of constipation, and have made the suitable purchases to appease everyone this side of the grave, we're still not home free. Have we betrayed those in the Great Beyond by consigning them to leaky coffins?

Commercial exploitation of patriotism goes back at least a century. Witness the contemporary sketch of a Centennial parade in Philadelphia, 1876. Still familiar today is the ad's accusatory tone: any mother who doesn't buy a certain brand of heating oil doesn't care if her babies burn to a crisp.

An easy-answers-to-insoluble-problems approach endows Eno's Fruit Salts with the ability to end the world's major ills, such as war and "outraged nature." For all its profuse name-dropping, the ad never makes the slightest connection between the dyspepsia remedy and "Human Nobleness!"

Engendering guilt feelings in the bereaved reaches a near-sadistic level in this ad, the cross-sectional view of the water-logged casket being particularly ghoulish. After all that, the solace the manufacturer offers in the copy is negligible.

Exaggerated claims for products go sometimes to extraordinary lengths, but few have gone as far as this 1891 example. Generous doses of Ayer's nostrum would cure not only a multitude of personal afflictions but also lingering post-Civil War bitterness between North and South.

This liquor ad induces, in the male, anxiety to the point of paranoia and a challenge to revolt. Buy the "right" brand and show *her* who's boss.

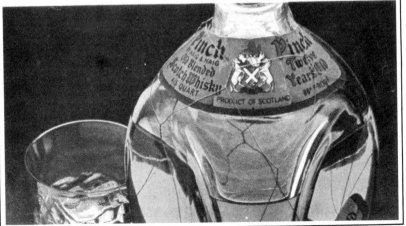

The nirvana-world of kitsch imagines an existence without problems, without difficulties, without inconvenience. In the lingo of the 1960s, all impediments to instantaneous happiness are reduced to "hassles." The tampon confers on the user both immediate membership in the Now Generation and automatic romance.

Introducing the hassle* free tampon.

Introducing the Kotex Natural Tip tampon. Simple, natural, hassle-free internal protection.
*No hassles with tubes.
The Kotex Natural Tip slips into place with neat little sticks instead of big and clunky tubes.
*No hassles with hard, blunt ends.
Our new Natural Tip is delicately tapered. It's very easy. And gentle on your body.
*No hassles with protection.
Only the Natural Tip gives you hours of Kotex protection. Not even the leading tampon can promise you that.

California orange-crate labels are currently enjoying a vogue among collectors, and many of the lithographs are striking pop art. However, this label (10"x11") is another instance of a product's dragging in an innocent bystander as witness. Here, Honest Abe lends a reverential—and irrelevant—tone to citrus fruit.

WASHINGTON NAVELS

LINCOLN BRAND

GROWN AND PACKED ON ARLINGTON HEIGHTS BY VICTORIA AVENUE CITRUS ASSOCIATION RIVERSIDE RIVERSIDE CO. CAL.

Sunkist

If Mozart were alive today, he'd be recording on "Scotch" brand recording tape.

Mozart was a child prodigy.   a hint from the master.

Fresh squeezed juice.
You remember what that is, don't you?

For all the working of the Pabst insignia into rosettes of Gothic tracery, summoning up of Cologne Cathedral, and Gretchen at her spinning wheel, it's still beer. Call this presentation of a bucket of suds High Culture Kitsch.

The awesome splendor of the blood-drenched Colosseum *(lower left)* provides a gruesome setting for peddling bedspreads. The ad suggests that the purchaser will move Rome's grandeur and Italy's art right into his own bedroom. At the very least, he is led down the Appian Way to believe, incorrectly, that the coverings come from Italy.

Reverse—or With It—Kitsch. Unlike the beer and the bedspread ads, this one *(lower right)* tries to deglamorize the most venerable and magnificent hotels in Italy; for example, Rome's Excelsior and Venice's Danieli and Gritti Palace. "Don't feel threatened by all that highbrow art. Honest, we're just like your home-town Hilton."

MILWAUKEE BEER IS FAMOUS PABST HAS MADE IT SO.

Can't Sleep?

Here is a truth you should know. A truth for the weary mind. If you take

PABST MALT EXTRACT The Best Tonic

you will drop off to restful slumber the minute your head touches the pillow. It................

Brings Strength

It quiets the nerves, and rounds the form, builds, braces and lifts the body and brain from weakness to power.. Gives youthful vigor. To win back health take............

Pabst........
Malt Extract
The "Best" Tonic

THE ART OF BREWING WAS DEVELOPED BY THE GERMANS

**Works of art from Italy.
Sears Bellissimo bedspreads.**

*When you ring
for room service
in a Doge's palace,
you know you're
in a CIGA Hotel.*

DVX ANDREA GRITTI

This painting of Doge Andrea Gritti still hangs in his 14th century Venetian palace. Only today, it's a CIGA Hotel. That's why we added our white push-button box to his portrait. As a reminder that, glamorous as the history of our hotels may be, we surround you with the most up-to-date comforts and conveniences. Push these buttons and people happen. The room maid, waiter or valet. Right at your guest room door because they're stationed on your floor. So it goes in every resplendent CIGA Hotel. Everywhere we are in Europe. Personal service without parallel in very luxe and lavish settings. Ask your travel agent. He'll tell you. Not every CIGA Hotel started as a palace. But the treatment is always royal. (And ask about our CIGA Venice Club. Free membership is open to any guest at one of our 6 Venetian hotels, and brings

Announcing the brand new 200-year-old collection: Spirit of '76 from Magnavox.

Independence Hall, Knott's Berry Farm, Buena Park, C

Happy birthday, America! You're going to be 200 years old.

And to help celebrate the bicentennial, Magnavox has designed a collection of home-entertainment products that faithfully recaptures the spirit of Revolutionary days.

A. Dry Sink (Model 6464). Authentic Early American styling hides stereo FM/AM radio-phonograph, 8-track tape player, 4-channel decoder and four speakers.

B. Blanket Chest (Model 6461). Replicas of Pennsylvania Dutch folk art and dovetails designed around stereo FM/AM radio-phonograph, 8-track tape player, 4-channel decoder and four speakers.

C. Queen Anne (Model 6465). Graceful cabinetry conceals stereo FM/AM radio-phonograph, 8-track tape player, 4-channel decoder and four speakers.

D. Spice Chest (Model 6455). Space-saving design enhances stereo FM/AM radio, 8-track tape player, 4-channel decoder and four high-efficiency speakers.

E. The STAR™ System (Model 4895). The most significant TV breakthrough since color: instant access remote-control tuning — by computer.

Get the Spirit today, at your Magnavox dealer. It's a beautiful way to take pride in our nation's heritage — and your home.

What a difference living with a Magnavox.

According to this ad, it's not so much a home-entertainment center that you'd be buying as a slice of Americana. The cabinetry is acceptably 18th-century style, perhaps, but the pieces are still only pseudo-antiques. In addition, it's hard to see how one celebrates the nation's Bicentenary with a stereo in a reproduction case with grill cloth sides. The ad further beguiles the buyer by invoking a reproduction of Independence Hall, located at Knott's Berry Farm, Buena Park, California.

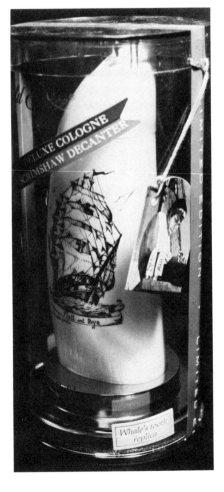

In the heyday of the great whaling industry, before the discovery of petroleum, sailors braved the dangers of the sea to bring back oil to light America's lamps. During the long months aboard ship, they carved whale's bones and teeth into canes, doorknobs, chessmen, clothespins, pie-crust sealers, rolling pins, and corset stays with finely incised designs of whaling scenes, patriotic emblems, and the faces of their wives or sweethearts to present as gifts when they returned home. Those scrimshaw articles are among the most treasured primitive-art items of America's past. The dandified plastic cologne bottle, shaped like a whale's tooth, with its machine-stamped ship and plastic red, white, and blue ribbons ballyhooing it as "Deluxe" and as a "Limited Edition," purveys one more piece of kitsch as a supposed tribute to American culture. (8")

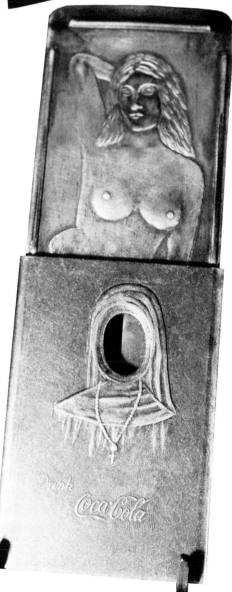

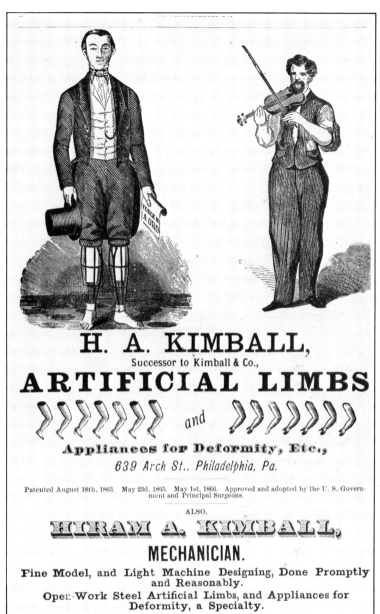

H. A. KIMBALL,

Successor to Kimball & Co.,

ARTIFICIAL LIMBS

))))) *and*)))))

Appliances for Deformity, Etc.,

639 Arch St.. Philadelphia, Pa.

Patented August 18th, 1863. May 23d, 1865. May 1st, 1866. Approved and adopted by the U. S. Government and Principal Surgeons.

ALSO,

HIRAM A. KIMBALL,

MECHANICIAN.

Fine Model, and Light Machine Designing, Done Promptly and Reasonably.

Open-Work Steel Artificial Limbs, and Appliances for Deformity, a Specialty.

Descriptive Circulars sent Free.

Kitsch can sometimes arise out of a clash of sensibilities. We don't know whether to laugh or weep at the dignified gent parading around in cutaway, top hat, and rolled-up trousers revealing his see-through legs and artificial feet. And the decorative row of un-attached arms and legs strikes a note of unintentional whimsy. Sometimes, a tactful reticence is welcome.

Early in this century, the Coca-Cola Company, among other firms, issued a series of men's bronze buckles to advertise its product. Most of the ornamental designs featured women, from the American opera singer Lillian Nordica to Amazonian nudes. By far the kitschiest trouser belt buckle was this one depicting two views of a nun. (2½" x 4", closed)

**The story of a girl who falls in love
with the world's greatest obscene phone call.**

This brochure promoting a film, *The Telephone Book* (1971), proves that for obscenity, right-on nudity can't compare with kitsch's smirking sidling up to it.

Who is the Olivetti girl?

And why are people saying such terribly nice things about her.

The Olivetti girl is a secretary/typist who's been attracting lots of attention lately for her amazing performance on the typewriter. Because no matter how fast she types she rarely makes a mistake! Now, she may be prettier than other typists, but she's not necessarily any brainier.
Then what makes an Olivetti girl such a phenomenal typist? Her brainy Olivetti Electric Typewriter, of course! This typewriter can actually think for itself. Because it has a brain inside that makes the four most common typing mistakes absolutely impossible. No flying caps!
    No improper spacing!
    No shading or ghosting!
    No crowding or piling!
That's why an Olivetti girl can really belt it out. And is sharper, looser, never uptight. That's why an Olivetti girl has more fun. And _that_ is why people are saying such terribly nice things about her.

olivetti
The Beautiful Dream Machines

office typewriters
portable typewriters
calculators
accounting machines
adding machines
electronic billing systems
microcomputers
computer terminals
office copiers

P.S. to Office Managers:
You never have to overspend for an Olivetti Electric Typewriter! Because we have six different models, each matched priced from $265 to $705, each matched to a specific secretarial work load. (Did you know that mismatched typewriters are costing American business millions of dollars a year?)
To get more information, see the Yellow Pages for the nearest Olivetti office.

The answer to a businessman's prayer: a good-looking, brainy typewriter that gets the work done and a pretty, if addled, secretary who dresses up the office. Because women are supposedly incompetent anyway, forget about intelligence and settle instead for a fun package that stays loose. As usual, solid virtues—the kind that men value—reside in a product. (1972)

CHAPTER 6

A Set of Building Blots

Unshapely mansions and other sites
too humorous not to mention

A traveler in Kitschland will observe that the territory is not neatly circum-scribed. Shifting perspectives can alter the boundaries. Nowhere is this clear-er than in the region of architecture, where, depending on the point of view, one man's castle can be taken for another man's kitsch.

In the early 18th century, certain German and British arbiters of taste took a holiday from the Age of Enlightenment and its neoclassical strictures gov-erning balance and harmoniousness in art, music, and literature. They look-ed to the past for a simpler way of life, much the way some of us today yearn nostalgically for "the good old days" of the Thirties, Forties, or Fifties. The Middle Ages, they found, offered a pleasing mixture of barbarism and super-stitious belief, and an invitation to visit the wilder shores of the imagination. In short, the Gothic Revival cultivated a preference for mystery and dark melancholy over reason and bright optimism.

Horace Walpole, author of *The Castle of Otranto* (1764-65), the first Gothic "horror" novel, was among the most influential of the British self-styled medievalists. In 1747, he built what he called "a little Gothic cas-tle," an imitation of a Gothic abbey adapted into an elaborate and com-fortable country residence. Strawberry Hill, as Walpole named the estate, in Twickenham, exerted an enormous influence on subsequent architecture.

Little less than a century later in America, Gothic buildings—often adorn-ed with slim roof pinnacles, tracery over arched windows, and crenelated door canopies—no longer suggested eccentric barbarism. Instead, they rep-resented the very height of sophisticated taste. Stimulated by the strange and rugged charm of the Gothic aesthetic, private citizens and public ad-ministrators commissioned architects to provide a required medieval at-mosphere. By the middle of the 19th century, American Gothic had taken root across the land, sprouting up in quaint and imposing forms as varied as country cottages and urban mansions, churches, prisons, libraries, fire houses, post offices, and railroad stations.

Today, we look on those capricious Gothic-inspired structures with con-descending amusement. But for all its sometimes cloying fancifulness, gin-gerbread Gothic pretends to be nothing more than it is, a decorative style adapted to latter-day needs and taste. It's only when the buildings pretend to be what they are not that they become kitsch. For example, the exterior walls of the Gothic-style First Parish Congregational Church in Brunswick, Maine, are "reinforced" by bogus buttresses ending several inches above the ground to prevent their rotting in rain puddles. Of a later date, and even more strikingly kitschy, is Harkness Memorial Tower, at Yale University in New Haven, Connecticut, a colossal piece of Hollywood modern Gothic, thoughtfully antiqued with preworn steps and artfully arranged moss on its roof.

It's absurd to fulminate against architectural styles such as Gothic Revival, although militant modernists made it fashionable to do so a generation ago. A style in itself isn't kitsch, but an outrageously or laughably inept use of it in a particular building may be.

Of course, imitation of architectural forms or elements doesn't necessarily result in kitsch. In this regard, it's instructive to consider the American Greek Revival style of the 1820s and 1830s, with its spacious white-columned porticos and façades "supported" by Corinthian pilasters. Not even the most fastidious purist would call it kitsch. Yet in 1835, Alexis de Tocqueville, that first and most judicious observer of the collision of art and mass appetite in America and an early prophet of kitsch, implied as much when he commented on New York's Greek Revival buildings. In a mass culture, he wrote,

the productions of artists are more numerous, but the merit of each production is diminished. No longer able to soar to what is great, they cultivate what is pretty and elegant, and appearance is more attended to than reality.

When I arrived for the first time at New York...I was surprised to perceive along the shore, at some distance from the city, a number of little palaces of white marble, several of which were of classic architecture. When I went the next day to inspect more closely one which had particularly attracted my notice, I found that its walls were of whitewashed brick, and its columns of painted wood. All the edifices which I had admired the night before were of the same kind.

It's risky to disagree with Tocqueville; doubtless there was something presumptuous about young America's attempt to re-create ancient Athens on the shores of the East River. However, Greek Revival architecture and the neoclassical style of Empire dress were but a new nation's outward show of an honest emulation of Athenian democratic ideals. The painted wooden pillars and whitewashed "palaces" may not have constituted great architecture, but they were visual tokens attesting to the equality of all free men, from modest shopkeepers to landed aristocracy. That bond between symbol and reality distinguishes Greek Revival from the kitschily ludicrous pretentions of Mussolini's self-aggrandizing efforts to restore the grandeur that was Imperial Rome by means of gleaming Neoclassical-Modernistic buildings and sculpture that appeared to be hewn from great cakes of soap. The Sam Rayburn Building, in Washington, D.C., embodies an even emptier, if less insidious, pomp.

Architectural kitsch often has the desperate air of someone who, eager to create a striking impression, both speaks and dresses too loudly. "Look at my fantastic clothes, my fabulous hair style, and my out-of-this-world jewelry. Aren't you staggered at the thought of what it all must have cost?"

To see swaggeringly pretentious structures, you have only to drive along any American highway. Cast a passing glance at the link in the Howard Johnson's restaurant chain. As bland in design as in its cuisine, it attracts the hungry traveler by the comfortable familiarity of its vaguely colonial outlines. Look briefly at the innocent roadside diner, whose only claim to making you wince is the labored coyness of its sign: Eaton B. Merry's Steak House.

Now, looming ahead, is a tall, slanting cylindrical structure. Indeed, from a distance it could be a tottering silo. A bit closer, it looks almost like—

how can it be?—the Leaning Tower of Pisa. It's a tower built at a tilt, all right. It's a leaning Tower of Pizza, a superb example of inane architecture considerably shorter than the 180-foot-tall original, whose tiers of columned arches have been simulated with solid-painted arch-forms. Thus debased, that legendary site of Galileo's momentous discovery concerning the velocity of falling objects has come to mean to millions of Americans no more than a fast-food stop.

With a nod of recognition, you pass a restaurant in the shape of a monumental pineapple, combining kitsch's predilection for slavish and unimaginative imitation with its fondness for ludicrous gigantism. Just down the road is a sprawling, out-of-scale version of Mount Vernon, the revered Georgian plantation home of the Father of Our Country. More Godfather than Father, the façade behind the colonnade is "Sicilian" permastone incongruously punctuated by bay windows hung with cottage curtains. The main doorway, bordered by glass bricks, has a screen door vaunting a pink flamingo silhouette.

Ahead lies a difficult choice. But pass up The Camelot, a motel designed, with kitsch's characteristic muddle-headedness, as a medieval castle of nearly a thousand years later than King Arthur. (Besides, castle keeps were never noted for their abundance of creature comforts.) Instead, choose Missile Motor Inn, a piece of offensive architectural presumption. A vainglorious replica of the rocket that carried the first men to the moon invites our cheap participation in a heroic event. That reduction of scientific marvel to commercial doodad equates bedding down in comfort and safety with hurtling through perilous space.

By comparison, a twenty-foot Hawaiian hula girl atop a motel in Michigan is merely silly kitsch—alluring in summer, but a bizarre sight when snowdrifts pile up around the Polynesian dancer's grass skirt.

Growing out of no tradition as did the Gothic or Greek revivals, embodying no coherent use of planes, textures, and space, kitsch architecture strives only for flashy effect. The architect Ludwig Mies van der Rohe, expressing admiration for the true elegance of simplicity in style, said, "Less is more." Those who are prey to the visual stridency of kitsch glorify "more"; to them, it is "Too *much!*"

Georgian and Greek Revival buildings were generally structurally honest: pillars really supported weight, and domes spanned space. But in the American Gothic Revival, beginning about 1840, cheap wooden imitations of stone architectural elements were applied to buildings merely to dress them up in the latest fashion. Instead of sustaining ceilings, arches hung from them. Typical of that genre is the First Parish Church in Brunswick, Maine. The buttresses "supporting" the tower and transept are wooden, like the rest of the building, and hollow and nonfunctional. The detail pictured here shows the mighty buttresses terminating several inches above the ground, the kind of kitsch that often goes unnoticed. The holes bored in the base are added insurance against physical—though not cultural—rot.

One of the aesthetic problems of the skyscraper style is knowing how to stop. Apart from the anomalous colossal Georgianism of Philadelphia's New Custom House (1933), on the Delaware River, is the wedding-cake piling up of topper upon topper until (apparently) money, materials, and imagination are exhausted. Immense federalese eagles, concrete globes, urns, cartouches, hints of Greek temples, and lunette windows multiply until finally, more out of desperation than through inspiration, the top dwindles into a screen-covered chimney.

An example of official kitsch magnificence, the Rayburn Building, Washington, D.C. (1964), named for Sam Rayburn, long-time Speaker of the House of Representatives, tries to compensate for its bleak austerity by a sprinkling of Ionic pillars and pilasters. They add neither dignity nor grace to the behemoth, only predictable unimaginativeness.

All within a few miles of downtown Manhattan and all within a few blocks of one another, these houses illustrate some home buyers' low sales resistance to anything that looks "elegant," "exotic," or "extraordinary." Here, you can learn how to play mix-and-match Domestic Architectural Kitsch.

Take one basic shingled box, add plywood arches, one stuccoed brick buttress, a paneled plastic garage door, and call it Spanish.

Take the same basic box, apply a stucco crenelated façade, rustic permastone base, two paneled plastic front doors, and you get a duplex Norman keep.

Enlarge the box, add Cape Cod-cottage weathered shingles, a formal Federal broken pediment above the entrance, a few spindly columns, and you achieve Early American.

Borrow the bay window from the first house, the garrison front from the "Spanish" or "Norman" house, pillars from the "Early American" house, and the all-purpose Olde Time diamond window panes, add a Venetian porch lantern, and voilà— All-American International Kitsch.

Instant Switzerland, wherever the buyer of this "modular home unit" chooses to put down roots—in Florida, in the Arizona desert, or actually on a mountain site. That it only remotely resembles a Swiss chalet bothers no one at all, for ostentation, not taste, creates the market for domestic architecture not indigenous to its destined surroundings.

Thomas W. Lamb designed more than 300 entertainment palaces of the Golden Age, including New York's Rivoli, Capitol, and Hollywood (now Mark Hellinger) theaters. In 1926, Lamb brought ancient Karnak to Gotham with this ziggurat zinger built for the Knights of Pythias fraternal order. Polychrome Pharaohs survey the New York scene from lofty perches at the foot of temples whose giant lanterns double as chimneys for the building.

The new sixty-story John Hancock Tower (1973) in Boston, Mass., like the Tower of Babel, is an example of architectural hubris. Built by I.M. Pei & Partners to loom majestically above Henry H. Richardson's Trinity Church and McKim, Mead & White's Public Library in Copley Square, the building has become an embarrassment and an eyesore. As window after window has shattered, sheets of plywood and tarpaper have had to be installed, making the interloper the world's tallest shanty.

Kitsch architecture has found a warm welcome on American college campuses. A desire to steep the university in hallowed tradition and awesome grandiosity gripped James Gamble Rogers, the architect of Yale's Harkness Memorial Tower (1918). The seductive pastiche with its moss-covered roofs and artfully worn steps is so flamboyantly picturesque, in the true manner of kitsch, as to make the cathedral at Chartres seem disappointingly pallid by comparison.

Yale's Sterling Memorial Library (1931) exemplifies kitsch's other habit, the yoking together of wild incongruities. The Gothic-at-any-cost dogma of academe fights here a losing battle against the need to house 3.5 million books. The outcome of the clash resembles a grain elevator with a Gothic loading platform.

Megalomania Kitsch afflicts the wealthy as well as the middle class, but more flamboyantly. In the Gilded Age of the late 19th century, New York millionaires vied with one another in self-preening display. They built enormous summer homes at Newport, Rhode Island, which with false modesty they called "cottages." The Romanesque fortress with the mundane window shades was the pleasure dome of Charles W. Lippett. The Breakers, Cornelius Vanderbilt II's ostentatious Italian palazzo, was built between 1893 and 1895 by Richard Morris Hunt. Those overblown confections of balconies, balustrades, gilded nymphs, red-brocaded walls, and multicolored marble columns bedazzled the rich, but earned only the scorn of the young architect Louis Sullivan, who derided as "absurd" the discrepancy between French and Italian Renaissance palaces and the silk-hatted gentlemen who lived in them.

For twenty-five years before 1914, when the tycoon James Deering built Vizcaya on Biscayne Bay in Florida, he ransacked half a dozen great French and Italian houses. Medieval altars, a Roman sarcophagus turned into a fountain, a fireplace from Catherine de'Medici's chateau, a stone barge "floating" in the Bay, a "Venetian" canal and casino— every nook and cranny of the white coral mansion and the estate cry out for applause.

Of all the loot-filled kitsch palaces in America, the most notorious is La Casa Grande, William Randolph Hearst's 146-room lair at San Simeon, California. Begun in 1922, the house was still under construction when Hearst died in 1951. For all its priceless antiques, the excessive agglomeration of styles, periods, and scales creates an effect of the kitschiest mishmash of schlock.

America's highways and resort areas teem with sleazy kitsch architecture. The appeal of structures such as this one, near Provincetown, Massachusetts, depends largely on "classy" associations that the customer brings to these visual puns.

After the opening of the Hawaiian Islands to American trade in the early 1800s, the pineapple became a symbol of hospitality, often carved as finials on furniture such as chairs and four-poster beds. The pineapple reaches its overblown commercial apotheosis in this highway restaurant near Camden, New Jersey.

America's love affair with anything in the form of anything else can account for the famous Brown Derby on Wilshire Boulevard, in Los Angeles, California.

Architectural kitsch's occasionally disarming naiveté (even to the inclusion of wooden spoons) indulges a child's dream of a world full of treats and goodies. This roadside stand flourished near Berlin, Connecticut, in the 1930s.

Space-fever kitsch. This orbiting road sign for three local motels stands near the missile base at Cape Canaveral, Florida. Just another piece of structural junk on the horizon of the future.

Because this bookstore in New York's Greenwich Village caters to science fiction fans, it seemed a good idea to fashion it like a spaceship. To reduce the proposition to vivid kitsch absurdity, a shop specializing in medical texts should be got up as a giant artificial lung; one dealing exclusively in cookbooks would be housed in a mammoth stove.

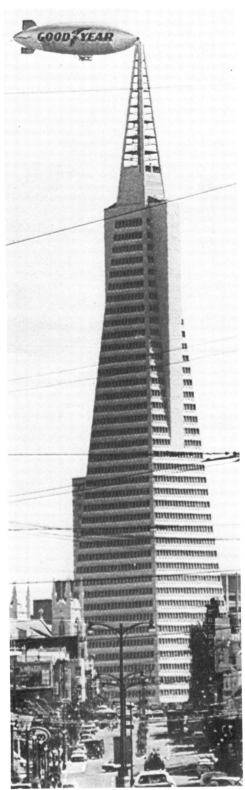

Neither an 853-foot-high oil derrick nor a mooring mast for dirigibles, but the Transamerica Pyramid, in San Francisco, California. Its outlandish design is rendered still worse by its total disregard for the scale of its surroundings. (The blimp, which appears to be tethered to the building, is actually several hundred feet beyond the structure.)

As a giant tank turret or a 230-foot cement bagel, Gordon Bunshaft's design might have been appropriate. But encountering the Hirshhorn Museum and Sculpture Garden (1974) on the bureaucratic Mall in Washington, D.C., one hardly knows whether to expect a howitzer, a computer card, or a piece of lox to pop out of the slot in its side. The nondescript style of the pinkish concrete pillbox has been dubbed "lumpengrandiosity" by *Time* and as "colossal funerary" by Ada Louise Huxtable, architecture critic of *The New York Times*.

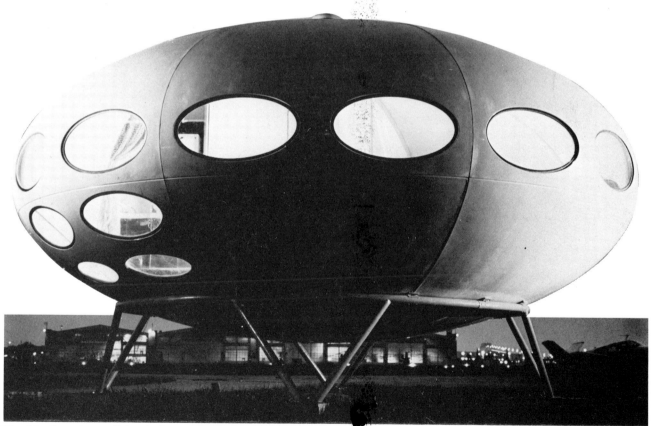

The Martians haven't landed—yet. Pausing at Philadelphia's International Airport on its way to permanent location somewhere in the United States, the Futuro II represents someone's dream house, vintage 1970. The trouble with up-to-the-minute architectural flights of fancy is that only a decade—or even a year—later they look as dated as a prop from Flash Gordon serials of the 1930s. Nothing dates faster than a kitsch idea of the future.

"The only elephant you can go through and come out alive" is how the Elephant Hotel in Margate City (near Atlantic City), New Jersey, disconcertingly bills itself. It was constructed between 1881 and 1885 by James V. Lafferty, who built similar ones at Cape May, N.J., and at Coney Island in Brooklyn, N.Y. *(right)*, both now demolished. The window under the tail of the 65-foot-high elephantine hotel, now undergoing renovation *(below)*, sums up the kitschiness of the odd—and delightful—enterprise.

Despite its pretensions, the Fontainebleau, at Miami Beach, Florida, qualifies as Monster Motel. Flanked by staggered setbacks, the curves of tiered accommodations suggest open-air cell blocks rather than the relaxed do-as-you-will ambience of a resort hotel. "Colonial" lampposts do their feeble best to add a dash of class and human proportion to this slick Vacation Machine.

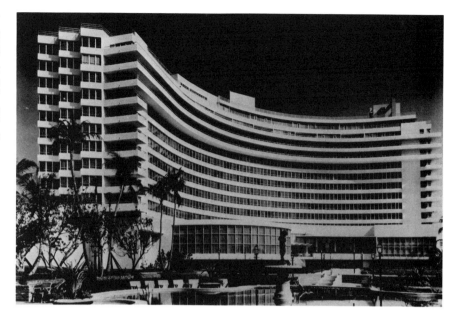

370. The Harvard School of Veterinary Medicine (built c. 1885), Village and Lucas Sts., Boston, Mass., c. 1889. [25]

Appropriateness, like irrelevance, can sometimes achieve ludicrous effects. Adaptation of the Romanesque arch to veterinary concerns accounts for the horse-collar doorway and top-floor niche of the Harvard School of Veterinary Medicine, built about 1885. The bull, seemingly peering out of a second-story window, serves as a gargoyle motif. The result is more endearing than imposing.

The Old South, but not so you'd recognize it. This is the lobby of the Regency Hyatt Hotel, on Peachtree Street, in downtown Atlanta, Georgia. Only a few years old, it has already gained a reputation as (a) one of America's most daring modern architectural splendors; (b) one of America's kitschiest modern architectural splendors. A revolving mushroom dome, in vertiginous aquamarine plastic, surmounts the luxurious lobby. From it hangs a spiky black metal sculpture. Lighted crystal-dome elevators soar to hanging garden balconies—red-carpeted, of course. An enormous fountain (not shown in the photograph), of chrome and glass tubing, beats like the heart of a giant robot.

Indians paddling on the River Thames? Guess again. You've heard of suckers buying the Brooklyn Bridge. The canny British managed to sell London Bridge to Lake Havasu City, where since 1971 the dignified structure has baked in the Arizona sun, amid the cactus and yucca.

Kitsch *trompe l'oeil* compensates for visual blight caused by other forms of urban kitsch. Unlike real scenery, "This Oregon scenaroma [*sic*] is for your viewing pleasure by courtesy of A-1 Electric & Plumbing Supply Co."

Hollywood Boulevard chinoiserie. The quintessence of gorgeously irrelevant architecture, Sid Grauman's Chinese Theatre opened in 1927. Such Ancient Egyptian, Turkish, Moorish, Italian baroque, and Chinese dream worlds, like most of the films they showed, fed the mass appetite for kitsch fantasy and adventure.

The Fox Theatre in Atlanta, Georgia, one of the most opulent movie palaces remaining in the United States, was built in 1929 at a cost of $4.5 million. Inspired by motifs of the Alhambra, it provides patrons with a Moorish courtyard setting for viewing movies taking place anywhere in the world, in any era. Improbable, but designed with flair and imagination, it represents kitsch at its most magnificently foolish. Castles in Spain, to be enjoyed for an hour or so—for the price of a ticket.

The corniest building in America is the pride and joy of Mitchell, South Dakota. Each year, two tons of many-colored corn on the cob are used to create new huge "paintings" on the exterior walls of the Corn Palace (1921). The picture "frames," the battlements and turrets, and all the architectural décor are made from thousands of bundles of a variety of grains. The sheer exuberance of the preposterous folk-art extravaganza, onion domes and all, makes this vegetable salad one of kitsch's rare appealing delights.

By day or night, the John F. Kennedy Center for the Performing Arts (1971) looks more like a gambling casino on the Potomac than a structure incorporating an opera house, a concert hall, and the Eisenhower and American Film Institute theaters. Like color-coordinated or thematic home decoration, Edward Durrell Stone's design is an example of timidity kitsch, the desire to appear respectable by total effacement of personality.

In its long history, the Great Sphinx of Giza has suffered all the neglect and destruction that man and nature could inflict. No indignity surpasses this magic-carpet transfer to Los Angeles, California. It stands as a perfect symbol of American kitsch exploitation—empty and for hire.

Neither a cuckoo clock nor the cottage of the Wicked Witch of the West, the Spadina House in Beverly Hills, California, was designed by Henry Oliver in 1925, and is still standing. Its straining for rustic cuteness and picturesque poverty marks it as fairy-tale kitsch.

CHAPTER 7

"...But I Know What I Like"

Furthering the coarse of art

Given the chance, kitsch displaces art much as bad money eventually drives out the good. Flashy, obvious, and exaggerated, it engages the senses in the immediate and uncomplicated way that candied apples attract youngsters. Like the syrupy coating that smothers the flavor of the fruit, kitsch stifles the infinite variations of response that the sounds, objects, and images of art can evoke. It replaces the subtlety and ambiguity of art with instantly recognizable stereotypes, or sensory neon signs that flash *How sad! How beautiful! How exciting!*

Apologists for kitsch insist that a Liberace or a Virgil Fox reveals the glories of piano or organ music to a multitude that otherwise would never experience the Deeply Satisfying Rewards of classical music. Once an appetite is awakened, the reasoning runs, the newly enlightened will by degrees eagerly move on to devour all Great Music.

However, it's not the substance that kitsch hustles but the manner and razzle-dazzle of presentation. Fox urges audiences into a cheering frenzy at his organ concerts by a formidable instrumental technique and by endearing himself to his youthful fans by proclaiming that he is "controversial as hell." In fact, the embellishment of surging swells and timber-shivering vibratos pouring forth from Fox's "Heavy Organ" arouses a craving not for more music by Johann Sebastian Bach but for still more throbbing and sonic overkill. Both Fox's organ and E. Power Biggs's recorded pedal-harpsichord treatments of Scott Joplin rags, however engaging, are as kitschy in their distortion of Joplin's piano pieces as Leopold Stokowski's pneumatic orchestral transcriptions of Bach's keyboard music. (Recordings of Debussy, as well as of Bach and Joplin, have been programmed from bloodless Moog electronic synthesizers—the contemporary American equivalent of the barrel organ. They're for anyone who covets kitsch.) By contrast, instrumentalists or conductors who serve the composer, rather than the audience, will seem pallid and inexpressive.

In the same way, those who delight at a miniature of Michelangelo's *Pietà* enhanced by a theatrical nimbus of blue glass and scarlet wounds, are in for a let-down if they ever see the actual work. No gold, no mirror, nor any blood to ooze. The only thing that would more deeply move those viewers is a supercharged kitsch *Pietà* equipped to pump a glistening red substance from the stigmata and tap-water tears from the blue-eyed Virgin Mary.

By blunting the senses through sensationalism, kitsch renders disappointing not only art but also life itself. Kitsch shares that quality with pornography. No flesh-and-blood lover can hope to match the marathon orgasms depicted in masturbatory fantasies. Similarly, what can you say about *real* twenty-five-year-old girls with incurable diseases—except that they can't

compare to Ali MacGraw, who died so beautifully in Ryan O'Neal's arms in *Love Story*.

Life is a rip-off in other ways. Why don't children have as many freckles as kids in Norman Rockwell's paintings? Why aren't real grandmothers, doctors, and counter clerks as friendly and sympathetic as Rockwell depicts them? Why can't actual people be as nice as they are in those pictures? Conversely, why don't children look as appealingly soulful as they do in Walter Keene's pictures of bug-eyed youngsters?

Kitsch displaces reality by a mawkish neverworld. Art informs, kitsch transforms.

Having elbowed its way into the presence of art, kitsch, like coarse and pushy Natasha in Chekhov's *Three Sisters*, soon begins to take over, giving orders and letting the servants know who is boss. Kitsch art tells us that we know not only what culture is but also how to put it to work. When it comes to useful art, the Old Master Italians win in a walkaway. Now, thanks to modern technology, we have copies of their paintings and statues —pretty nearly as good as the originals, if we're any judge. What's more, they can be useful as well as decorative. For starters, there's a *Mona Lisa* bath towel, a stunning and practical accent for the powder room and sure to excite envious comment. A pair of Michelangelo's *Davids* make dressy lamps for sofa endtables. (It's OK, they come with fig leaves.) The blessing of fine art is that it fits in everywhere. Art is universal, all right. That antacid commercial on TV, after all, uses theme music from the movie *2001: A Space Odyssey*, doesn't it?

One doesn't have to rely on the masters for art. All large cities, resorts, and art colonies have "galleries" filled with Original Oil Paintings. Those works are often displayed in categories according to predominant color so that a careful shopper can get one or two to blend with the decorative scheme of a room.

Although all the works are hand-painted, as advertised, they aren't as expensive as Old Masters because improved methods have brought down the price to within easy reach of the tightest budget. It stands to reason that art can be produced faster by many hands making light work. Companies hire facile specialists. If dwindling inventories indicate a fresh need for mountain-and-lake scenes, a sky painter does a variety of skies, from unclouded to lowering; a water expert works in the lakes, calm or rough; and a foliage specialist lays down the trees with appropriate greenery. Because they're all skilled artisans, they work efficiently; and the resulting savings, thanks to mass-production techniques, are passed on to the buyer. For those with more elevated taste, works in the style of Renoir, Picasso, Rouault, Dufy, Dali, and other Modern Masters are available in a wide range of subjects and colors.

The kitsch urge impels some people to produce their own great works. Instead of acquiring bad copies of masterpieces, they buy reduced-size plastic molds of many of the great statues, and even of paintings made three-dimensional. Then, with plaster of Paris, liquid plastic, or wax they find they can turn out their own art. If they're handy with paints and have a degree of imagination, they may improvise added decorative touches.

How nice it is to paint an Early American picture that you can call your own. No chance of slip-ups. Because all the paints and the areas on the cardboard are color-coded, a meticulous filler-in is guaranteed a genuine work of art that to him is indistinguishable from the original, except that it is in his home and not in a museum. Even the Metropolitan Museum of Art, in

New York, recently offered for $2,000 a four-by-six-foot embroidery kit of *The Unicorn in Captivity*, perhaps the most famous medieval tapestry. With practice, the copier should be able to create his own great art without guidelines. Why not? He's learned from experts.

To return to music, the thrift motive of kitsch works in yet another way. Hucksters on television promote records-by-mail. Misapplying what they know of rock-music and nostalgia fans, whose favorites run to two or three minutes playing time, they offer bargain-priced packages such as "100 Great Moments from Great Music." The idea behind pitches like this—besides that of making money—is, why should anyone waste time listening to the arty folderol that surrounds the catchy bits in the March from *Aida*, Beethoven's Fifth Symphony, *Swan Lake*, or *Finlandia?* Customers rest content that they have bought most of the important great music, and let it go at that. Once they've got the hummable melodies, redundancies such as variations and developments become time- and money-wasting.

If sophisticates should want more by the same composers, kitsch peddlers have provided them with *Beethoven's Greatest Hits* and *Sibelius's Greatest Hits*. Presumably, nobody would be interested in listening to works that aren't hits. Or in hearing composers not found worthy of prepackaging.

"Gee! This'll *make* Beethoven," Walt Disney exclaimed when he saw the *Pastoral* Symphony enlivened for a sequence of *Fantasia* (1940). That Beethoven regarded his symphony as "the expression of feeling rather than painting" failed to daunt the cartoon tycoon. Set down in a sylvan simulacrum of Greek mythology, the centaurs and Disney-invented *centaurettes* resemble, from the waist up, wholesome American college athletes and teenyboppers. Originally, the girls were topless—Disney's idea of Art—but the Hays Office prescribed garland halters to placate American taste. Even the boys were nippleless. All in all, the sequence was marshmallow-fluff kitsch.

John Rogers (1829-1904), self-professed purveyor of "art for the people," turned away from the sterile and frigid classicism of his day to a homespun realism. During a period of twenty years, he sold more than a hundred thousand of his plaster domestic and patriotic groups at an average price of $15 apiece. *Coming to the Parson* (22" high, 1870) was the most popular of his statuettes, selling more than 8,000 copies. Like their descendants, Norman Rockwell's saccharine narrative paintings, Rogers's heartwarming homilies are long on sentiment, short on art.

In 1832, when Horatio Greenough was commissioned by the United States Congress to create a heroic statue of George Washington for the Capitol rotunda, he fashioned this charade of the first president as the Olympian Zeus of Phidias. Even at the height of the Greek Revival, the periwigged figure looked more like a Turkish bath patron than a god, and the statue was relegated to a remote corner of the Capitol grounds. It is now on display at the Smithsonian Institution, in Washington, D.C.

◀ *Homage to Terpsichore* is the chaste title of the proscenium mural painted by Enrique Senis-Oliver, a Spanish artist, for New York's Harkness Theater, opened in 1974 as a home for the Harkness Ballet. A modestly cloaked Rebekah Harkness, artistic director and proprietor of the company, stands among a morass of fanciful male buttocks and real candelabra, the modern equivalent of the ripe female nudes that once adorned walls of saloons and brothels.

In a rushed world of competitive visual clutter, we don't "see" things so much as we identify them. Only by their amplification, repetition, or magnification can aural or visual images cut through the miasma. Thus, Andy Warhol singled out the Campbell's soup can, one of millions of "invisible" objects, and exploded it into an enormous painting (oil on canvas, 24"x36") in order to draw our attention to it as a piece, however banal, of structure, design, and color composition. (His eight-hour-long film of the top of the Empire State Building, *Empire* [1964], and his painting of repeated images of a man strapped in an electric chair use other means to produce the same impact.) Ironically, kitsch proliferation of Warhol's statement into soup-can coffee tables, wastebaskets, and coffee mugs (3¾") has returned the object to the hurly-burly from which the artist temporarily freed it.

110

America's preoccupation with the subject of weeping children is more a psychiatric than an artistic matter. During the 19th century, thousands of watercolors and embroidered pictures depicted tearful little girls flung across the graves of departed ones. A tear-jerking popular song early in this century portrayed an orphaned youngster telephoning Mommy in heaven. In these kitschy pictures of mournful girls and boys, only a prettified sweet misery of life remains. Even a cause for the grief they express has been wiped away. All the effort of reacting to the paintings has been spared the viewer; the reaction is built-in. That's what kitsch is all about. (5½"x7½"; 5½"x11½")

Art becomes just a plaything for idle hands. Kitsch gets it all together in a jigsaw puzzle of Grant Wood's painting, *American Gothic.* (18"x22½")

The American primitive oil painting (second quarter of the 19th century) reflects the artist's absorption in his subject. The scene convinces by its gradual revelation of three generations of a family and their firm anchoring in a time with a present (the father glancing at his pocket watch), a past (the painting, on the wall, of an earlier generation, also with twins), and an implied future (a young suitor and the daughter waiting to be won). The kitsch print (varnished, photographed, and mounted on pressed board) oozes self-conscious charm. From the modern china-doll faces to the out-of-place "antique" props (the bed covering used as a tablecloth, the bed warmer) and the aggressively cute cat, the picture is less a view of life than a condescending statement from artist to viewer about quaintness. (29½"x24¾"; 16"x20")

Cast in tinted wax and silvered, the *Venus de Milo* candle awaits consignment to the all-consuming flame of kitsch. Kitsch artistry can provide also a two-in-one bargain: Leonardo's *The Last Supper* and, on the candle's other side, Dürer's omnipresent *Hands of an Apostle.* (9½"; 8½"x5")

When the *Mona Lisa* became the world's Most Famous Painting or That Woman With the Enigmatic Smile, it became kitsch. It elicits an immediate response that has little to do with a subtle work of art. Everyone's token masterpiece, it has been smeared across china plates, beach towels, and T-shirts. This drawing-by-computer approximation has as little to do with Leonardo's painting as a Moog synthesizer has with a great organist's performance of Bach. As a map for a color-coded painting, the work becomes a toy to delude the applier of paint into thinking that he, too, is an artist. (36"x48", *detail;* 18"x24")

"Sculpturettes: Mini-replicas of world-renowned sculptures. Executed in an amazing new technique of durable plastic for the authentic glow of polished white marble. One of the most distinctive cake ornaments ever offered—Rodin's *The Thinker!*" (From a cake decoration catalog; 5½")

The appeal of primitive, or naive, art lies in its strength of line and bold planes of light and color, its firm grasp of the essence of the experience. (In that regard, naive art is a precursor of both Impressionism and Cubism.) The kitsch attraction of these contemporary do-it-yourself "primitive" plywood plaques is that they require no more talent than does a child's coloring book. Even with the machine-bored wormholes, they are as remote from the past as they are from art. (17"x12"; 12"x18")

Little nippers become neighborhood celebrities when they hold this battery-powered plastic trumpét (12") to their rosebud lips, "work the buttons any old way" (as the directions glibly direct), and "play" any of the twelve rousers provided with the toy, including "Reveille" and "I've Been Working on the Railroad." The pretense that children may produce "live" music by means of "dead" plastic instruments and discs underlines kitsch's contribution to cultural slumber.

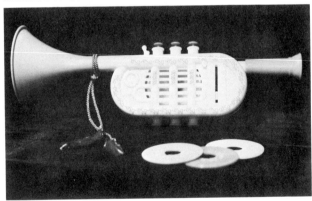

After spending hours incising the design into this plastic whale's tooth and rubbing black ink into the grooves, what you get is what you see—a piece of phony scrimshaw, decorated with a mass-produced design. The process is not creation, but kitsch make-believe; the result is schlock.

It may not be art or even credible history, but kitsch seldom comes in so lovable a form. This oil painting of a prairie traffic jam, by John Gast, a patriotic enthusiast of America's Manifest Destiny, is entitled *Westward Course of the Empire* (1872). The balloonlike apparition before whom the Indians flee may represent the blessings of civilization. As she strings telegraph wires across the continent, she clutches in her right arm a volume inscribed, with simple directness, *School Book.* (16"x12¼")

"ALL IS VANITY"

A perennial favorite with the shudder-loving set since its appearance in the early 1900s, *All Is Vanity* still knocks them dead when displayed in den, bar, or rumpus room. The drawing is often mistaken for Art, but its morbidly pretentious moralizing qualifies it better as kitsch. Charles Allan Gilbert (1873-1929), a native of Hartford, Connecticut, and a prolific illustrator, backed himself into a one-work corner when he produced this grisly optical trick. (10"x13")

On a more sophisticated, and pretentious, level, realism and allegory combine again to produce kitsch. This cenotaph (52') by Hermon Atkins MacNeil (1866-1947), is one of a pair flanking the Benjamin Franklin Parkway, in Philadelphia, Pennsylvania. It was erected in 1926 to commemorate naval heroes of the Civil War. The grouping, with its patriarchal leaders, saintly wounded martyrs, and angelic youths, is no worse than most official kitsch art. But the clash of romantic realism, the pylon's Art Deco bas-relief figure, and the post-office art eagle and dolphins raise the monument to the very heavens of pompous kitsch.

The classics prove their ability to hack it in the marketplace. Who knows? With a little more savvy Bach, Mozart, and Satie themselves might have written great pop and rock hits. Fortunately, along came Jethro Tull, Waldo de los Rios, and Blood, Sweat & Tears.

Like language reduced to cliché, art dies when it becomes nothing but lazy journalistic metaphor. The mighty figure of the Pharaoh Khafre, which the ancients recognized as one of the Seven Wonders of the World, has become an illustrator's all-purpose symbol of enigma and inscrutability.

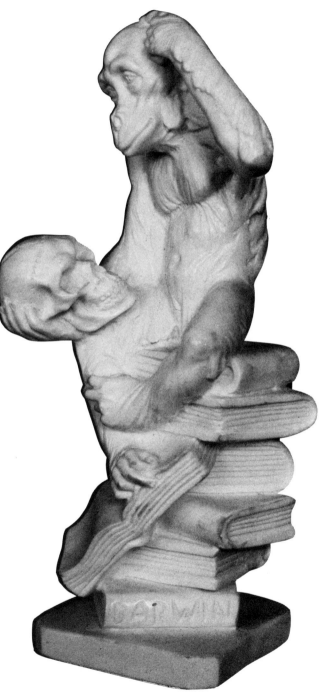

Both Rembrandt's painting *Aristotle Contemplating the Bust of Homer* and Darwin's epochal theory of evolution are reduced to drivel in this plaster kitsch aping of art. (8″)

The kitsch plot thickens as the literary works are diluted into comic books. Mood, style, and characterization vanish in these quickie bastardizings. Far from whetting appetites for the real thing, they merely induce dissatisfaction with the long-winded originals.

Worse and more of it. In this 1934 Big Little Book (companion to stories about Mickey Mouse, Little Orphan Annie, and Dick Tracy), there are all of seventy-five pages of text, none of it from Herman Melville—not even the plot. It's based not on his novel, but on a silent-movie version, *The Sea Beast* (1926), with John Barrymore. In this kitschy, upbeat improvement, Captain Ahab, far from perishing in his unsuccessful pursuit of the White Whale, kills it and returns safely to the waiting arms of a sweetheart named, not surprisingly, Faith. (5"x5")

When the United States Post Office chose James McNeill Whistler's *The Artist's Mother: Arrangement in Grey and Black* for the design of the Mother's Day stamp in 1934, the painter's simple, eloquent austerity was prettied up by President Franklin Roosevelt's addition of a pot of carnations. The perpetrator of the Geophysical Year stamp (1957) clearly wanted something momentous to commemorate that event. What more fitting subject than Michelangelo's Sistine Chapel ceiling, from which these arms were amputated, then rendered in Halloween-pumpkin orange? The 1940 series of stamps honoring great American composers ignored Louis Moreau Gottschalk and George Gershwin but not Ethelbert Nevin, composer of *My Rosary* and a setting of Eugene Field's poem "Little Boy Blue." In 1940, even the kitsch-gorged public derided the absurd use of the Three Graces, from Botticelli's *Primavera,* to honor the Pan-American Union. Michelangelo's sculptures *Bound Captives* never had an odder job than holding aloft, on this 1902 stamp, electric light bulbs, in tribute to Benjamin Franklin.

Simulation kitsch. Commissioned for the opening, in 1971, of the John F. Kennedy Center for the Performing Arts, Leonard Bernstein's *Mass* attempts to fuse Roman Catholic tradition with rock music, through imitation of externals. The strained effects waver between ponderousness and Boston "Pops" jive, patronizing both classical music and the authentic sound of the Youth Generation. *Mass* neither coheres nor convinces. The composer is shown at the premiere, wearing tuxedo and priestly stole.

CHAPTER 8

The Showy Must Go On

An excursion into excesses in films, fairs, and other show-biz happenings

It's often assumed, though it has never been shown, that restraint results necessarily in Good Taste. Minimally furnished living space; skyscraper façades bare of ornamentation, either pleasing or ugly; and formal attire that doesn't jumble saddle shoes with tuxedos must inevitably evince good taste because they practice restraint.

Possibly. But before passing judgment, it's important to know how well appointed are those uncluttered rooms; what, in fact, the safely unadorned building looks like; and what are current mandates governing sartorial excellence. If assembled elements, however few of them may compose a form, nevertheless produce an effect of excess, then kitsch rears its protean head.

Show business, the entertainment arts in general, is one thing. Show biz, when it prods us to match our response to its exploitative excesses, is another. Probably no one, neither layman nor theologian, has criticized the Lord's Prayer on the grounds of poor taste. (Except, perhaps, W. Somerset Maugham; in his novel *The Razor's Edge*, he presents a case for regarding that passage from the book of Matthew as childishly egocentric and tastelessly anthropomorphic.) As set to music in the thirties by Albert Hay Malotte, an American composer, the prayer may move some to tears and others to smiles. But when Ed Sullivan, as host of a weekly television variety show, came back on stage after a performer's rendition of the Malotte song to jab the studio audience with "Let's hear it for the Lord's Prayer!", his superfluous wheedling and the spectators' dutiful whoop-up for the solemn petition that Jesus taught his disciples adds up to more than the sum of the parts to produce vulgar excess. That's not just entertainment, that's show-biz kitsch.

Large spectacles such as world's fairs and expositions are generous contributors to the nation's storehouse of kitsch. Hideously elaborate structures, such as the fantasy-French Empire Temple of Music constructed for the 1901 Buffalo Pan-American Exposition, or monstrously outsize sculptures have provided our fairs with grotesque, if ephemeral, examples of unrestrained and inharmonious design. The colossus of George Washington that loomed over part of the 1939 New York World's Fair seems not to have been so much an imposing tribute to the first president of the United States as it was a googol golem. Sixty-five feet high, it was aesthetically as well as physically dwarfed by the geometric beauty of the fair's twin focal point, an enormous sphere adjoining a three-sided, tapering pylon that soared 700 feet, serenely dominating the 1,200-acre exhibition site.

Both the statue of Washington and the Trylon and Perisphere were Midway attractions meant to awe and delight their audience. Each work was intended as an example of representation or abstraction. However, the pretentious size of one merely taxed belief and thus, paradoxically, limited response to it; the other, relating to nothing but itself, was admirable. One was show-biz kitsch; the other was show business, and perhaps art.

Of course, exaggeration is part and parcel of show biz. Without it, carnivals would be dreary affairs—no barkers pitching wild claims about the world's shortest, fattest, sexiest whatevers. Circuses would be one-dimensional, black-and-white washouts deprived of garish costumes, of frantic activity in not one—not two—but three rings, and without big brass bands that could pulverize the walls of Jericho. But mere exaggeration isn't kitsch, any more than show business is necessarily show biz. Or any more than "Let's hear it for a great singer—Sergio Franchi!" would have been the same as Sullivan's "Let's hear it for the Lord's Prayer!"

Overstatement is the lifeblood of Hollywood's historical spectaculars. However, kitsch lurks among the thrones and throngs. We expect ancient Babylonian, Egyptian, or Roman settings to overwhelm us with richly exotic décor and trappings, and no elephantine epic worth its incense has disappointed us, from the monumental royal court of Belshazzar in D.W. Griffith's *Intolerance* (1916) through Cecil B. DeMille's palace of Rameses in *The Ten Commandments* (1923, 1956) to Rome welcoming Egypt's queen in Joseph L. Mankiewicz's *Cleopatra* (1963). Thou shalt reveal to the multitude, runs the Eleventh Commandment, the magnificence of monarchs amid a splendor of cumbersome costumes and of colonnades that glisten like gargantuan dentures.

Griffith's naively boastful delight in interrupting the action of some of his films with a flashed announcement of how much the scene cost heaps pretension upon ostentation. That information may fascinate film historians, and probably would have pleased Bertholt Brecht, who used such distancing, or "alienating," devices in his plays. But for most of us, the interpolation is gratuitous, and smacks of the swagger of kitsch.

To DeMille and his disciples in the movie business, the ancient world was a series of prurient pagan cultures. All of them were doomed because they had the bad luck to flourish B.C., or before Jesus' teachings had time to spread, and because they were preoccupied with sex. DeMille and others portrayed that moral deficiency in obligatory orgy scenes, with couples not only sprawling and writhing picturesquely on tables and great staircases, but also devouring grapes, Hollywood's shorthand for lewd behavior. Worse still—they nibbled the fruit directly off the bunch! That *reductio ad absurdum* depiction of depravity at its nadir is the reverse of show-biz excess, but is no less an example of simplistic kitsch.

Certain show-biz "events" are inherently kitschy. One such category is splashy and meaningless record-setting, whether of flagpole sitting, goldfish swallowing, or intrusive streaking. Foremost among such exploitative non-events were the dance marathons of the 1930s, in which the instinct that popularized the lions-versus-Christians sport in ancient Rome compelled hordes of torture buffs to watch Depression-poor couples flail themselves into exhaustion and collapse in a manic attempt to win meager cash prizes.

More gaudy and pretentious are beauty pageants. In those surrogate slave auctions, scores of pneumatic, plastic, and disposable human Barbie Dolls with vacuous faces and fixed smiles parade before judges, and millions of television oglers, to vie for the title of that year's Miss Forgettable. The stripper's runway is negotiated and the fannies are oscillated to Bert Parks's gushy commentary that swathes the exhibitionism in whole-cloth tales about talent, culture, and the Miss America dream of success.

Somewhere between Coleridge's "willing suspension of disbelief" and P.T. Barnum's "There's a sucker born every minute" lies the unabashedly preposterous world of show-biz kitsch.

✭☆✭☆✭☆✭☆✭☆✭☆✭☆✭☆✭☆✭☆✭☆✭☆✭

One of the liveliest attractions of Chicago's Columbian Exposition of 1893 was a wriggling exotic dancer who brought a whiff of pseudo-Oriental sexual mystery to midland America. From Little Egypt in the Gay Nineties to the belly-dance revival of the Swinging Seventies, hootchy-kootchy kitsch has exposed its bare midriffs, with veiled references. (The itchy fingers of censorship removed Little Egypt's navel from her photographs.)

Contrasts in public exhibition styles. Buffalo's Pan-American Exposition, held in 1901, offered a look of antiquity, with reveries of triumphal pylons and nightmares of Beaux-Arts furbelows, such as the Pantheon-inspired Temple of Music, site of President William McKinley's assassination. By contrast, the New York World's Fair of 1939 displayed "The World of Tomorrow." The values of things to come were kitsch's time-honored ones, money and cultural veneer. The bright red, revolving cash register, exalted on a pedestal, tallied the Fair's daily box-office receipts. The sixty-five-foot colossus of George Washington was meant, by its sheer mass, to impart a tone of reverent solemnity to the show-biz event.

123

Babylon outdone. D. W. Griffith's *Intolerance* (1916), one of the seminal works of cinematic art, includes this fanciful palace of Belshazzar, no less kitschily improbable for its appearance in a masterpiece. In conceiving his design for the set, perhaps Griffith was recalling *Belshazzar's Feast* and *The Fall of Nineveh,* fussily Victorian, but wildly imaginative, paintings by John Martin (1789-1854), a British artist.

If there were no grapes, it would have been necessary for Hollywood to invent them. In depicting orgies from ancient times onward, movies included grape-nibbling as a fail-safe prelude to dalliance. In *Queen Christina* (1933), even Garbo, as the Swedish monarch, and John Gilbert, as a Spanish ambassador, do it as their amorous moment of no return approaches.

124

The Depression forced millionaires to peddle apples, and some down-and-outers found even more bizarre ways to make a dime. Across the country, paying customers crowded ballrooms to watch hungry couples dance themselves from numbed stupor to exhaustion and collapse. Dance marathons provided entertainment as well as prize money. If, after hundreds of hours of nonstop competition, contestants dropped dead from overexertion —well, they shoot horses, don't they?

Enjoying a respite from her cinemaquatic displays, Esther Williams parodies "Miss Whatever" contests in a scene from *Easy to Love* (1953). With its bathing-suited entourage and citrus throne, this spoof of a beauty contest points up the silliness of the real thing.

Only the annual Tournament of the Roses in Pasadena, California, could think of ways to use thousands on thousands of blossoms in its garishly kitschy floats. Entitled "The Voyage of Atlantis," this prize-winning concoction of porpoises and a giant clam shell provides a flowerbed for curvaceous beauties.

Not even Florenz Ziegfeld got the mileage out of chorus girls that Busby Berkeley did. In films, they formed provocative configurations such as this spread-legged fountain *(Footlight Parade,* 1933) and "The Hall of Human Harps" *(Fashions of 1934).* Berkeley's imaginative and lavishly staged production numbers made millions of movie fans happy, including those with a taste for kinky sex.

The crypto-lesbian overtones of female wrestling matches exert a perverse fascination for those who like their contact sports with a difference.

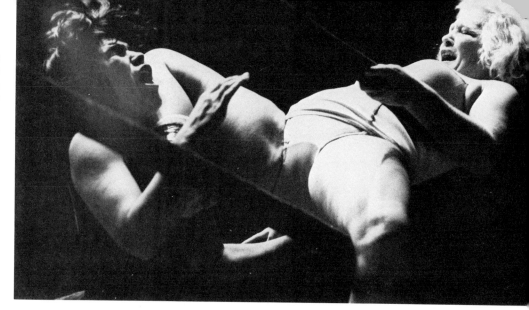

One of the biggest kitsch figures of television in the 1940s, Gorgeous George was a not-so-tough wrestler who pampered his curly locks with a spun-gold hairnet and never began his routine unless Jeffrey, his valet, had first perfumed the mat. The all-in-fun wrestling stints may have been fake, but the peroxide that George used on his hair was real.

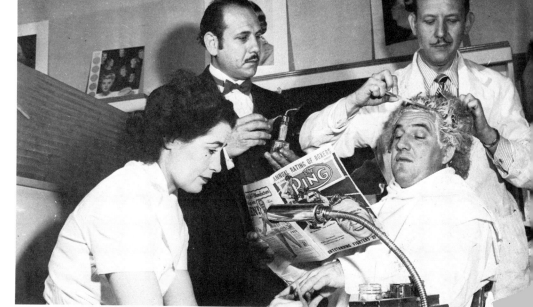

Radio City Music Hall's spectacular Easter show is an annual New York kitsch tradition. In a 36 Beautiful Virgins 36 precision strut, the Rockettes parade piously to the strains of Anton Rubinstein's *Kammenoi-Ostrow*. For an impressive finale, they form a human cross, their arms laden with Easter lilies. The tableau, shown in this souvenir program, never fails to bring down the house.

Walt Disney created an enchanting world populated with pert mice, irascible ducks, and, in *Snow White and the Seven Dwarfs,* an enduring cinematic achievement. But inflate that dream world into actuality, "people" it with grotesquely literal, larger-than-life replicas of those cartoon characters, strew it over hundreds of acres called Disneyland (at Anaheim, California) and Disneyworld (in Orlando, Florida) and the magic evaporates into real-estate ventures on a gigantic scale. When Disneyland opened in July 1955, its creator appeared on national television to announce that the sprawling playground "will never be completed, as long as there is imagination left in the world." Although both of the resorts are enormously successful business enterprises, they lack nevertheless what Keats called "the truth of Imagination."

Beneath the neon razzle-dazzle, gambling casinos, and star-studded cabarets of Las Vegas, Nevada, lies a tacky world of avarice and self-destructive pleasure.

128

Souvenirs level all significant experiences—Grand Canyon, the battlefield at Gettysburg, one's own wedding—to a series of schlocky checklists of accomplishments. The externalizing of memories into knickknacks, stamped with place and time— lest we forget our memorable experiences—is pure kitsch. The New York World's Fair of 1964, a tinseled international carnival, produced these tin-tray memory joggers.

To some stern critics of popular culture, pop songs are a species of kitsch—obvious and sentimental in their idealizing of romantic love. For decades, Lawrence Welk's hackneyed, ah-one, ah-two, ah-three renditions have spun out an endless flow of flat ginger ale, rather than champagne.

The demand of kitsch is always for increasingly breathtaking effects. The Hollywood ethos, as manifested in the movie spectacular, is a perfect embodiment of that "stronger wine and madder music" impulse. Each new film incarnation of ancient Rome requires more and more rows of columned temples, gleaming like a false-teeth exhibit. The ultimate in marmoreal kitsch dullness was reached in *Cleopatra* (1963). Arrayed in scrupulously researched Cleopatran garb, Elizabeth Taylor here descends upon Rome, every inch the Queen of Hollywood.

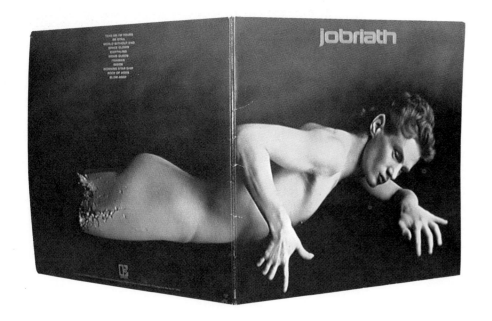

Jobriath's debut record album prophetically pictured him as a toppled, broken idol. One of many ephemeral glitter-rock stars, he employs calculated transvestism and professed homosexuality to exploit his audience's fascination with the forbidden. Resplendent in magenta lipstick and robin's-egg-blue body tint, Jobriath is self-conscious kitsch.

A best-selling record in 1973, John Wayne's *America, Why I Love Her,* brought a lump to some throats, but stuck in the craw of others. A rhymed, sentimental valentine, the album seemed more a jingoist apology for the Viet Nam war ("Why Are You Marching, Son?") than a recital of the nation's self-evident glories.

The ancient Egyptians ensured the immortality of the Pharaohs by building pyramids. The Roman emperor Caligula appointed his horse a consul. In Hollywood, fame is enshrined in wet cement. Preserved for the ages in the sidewalk outside Grauman's Chinese Theatre are the names of Wallace Beery, Joan Crawford, and Shirley Temple, as well as impressions of Betty Grable's legs and a sketch of Jimmy Durante's nose. In 1938, Charlie McCarthy set his wooden feet among the immortals, with the help of his spokesman, Edgar Bergen. "Trigger," Roy Rogers's palomino stallion, put his best hoof forward in 1949.

There'll always be a glamorously extravagant Hollywood—or so we once believed. Toward the end of its palmy days, Natalie Wood, a child actress in 1947, puts the final touch on an $8,000 Christmas tree, overdressed with the skins of sixty-seven white mink.

131

Minstrel shows, both professional and amateur, have receded into the past. White men pretending to be black men made the latter objects of condescending humor.

Significantly, minstrel shows with black performers were never as popular as the black-face representations of shuffling, lazy, and rascally "coons."

Whom Louella Parsons has joined together... To the most celebrated and feared of Hollywood's gossip chroniclers, movie stars were "nothing more nor less than fiction characters come to life." Her selective dissemination of intimate—sometimes imaginary—details of their personal and professional lives fed America's insatiable appetite for peekaboo glimpses of their gods

and goddesses. Shortly after this publicity photograph was taken in 1939, Ronald Reagan and Jane Wyman (here being embraced by a motherly "Lolly") costarred in a marriage that ran several reels. The surrounding starlets, including Susan Hayward (*right*), await their turn to be brought to life by the powerful fairy godmother.

The early 1970s saw a revival of the goldfish-swallowing and panty-raiding syndrome. "Streaking," running nude down a street or into a crowded theater, was intended to produce shocks and thrills, two of kitsch's favorite responses. The now-faded fad, demonstrated here at the University of Missouri, in Columbia, barely drew giggles in this era of permissiveness.

Each week during its heyday in the 1950s, *This Is Your Life,* television brainchild of host Ralph Edwards (*left*), permitted America to play Peeping Tom. Awkward reunions among estranged family members, discomforted film stars welcomed back unexpectedly from successful bouts with alcoholism, and surprise parties for celebrities dumfounded in the presence of unremembered old acquaintances gave audiences the mildly sadistic thrill of seeing the unsuspecting caught off guard. Perhaps the oddest collection of guests was this troupe of "entertainers," flown in from Ecuador for a program in 1957: a missionary, a Shapra chief's family, and, to round out the glad occasion, a visitor from the savage Auca tribe, which had recently murdered the missionary's brother.

When the famous operatic soprano Eleanor Steber appeared at New York's Continental Baths, she sang arias by Mozart, Massenet, and Puccini. One observer hailed the event as "an affair to rank with the coming of Christ, the death of Garland, and the freezing of spinach!" Even Mayor John V. Lindsay extended his congratulations on the "black towel concert." Many came to worship the diva as a kind of Our Lady of the Steambaths. But the album, recorded "live" in 1973, turns Miss Steber's echoes of former opera-house triumphs into one of the kitsch events of the decade.

Aglow with glamor and glitter, Liberace brought gilded candlesticks, beaded jackets with ruffled cuffs, sly winks, and dimpled smiles to millions of television viewers. Most of them were plus-forty housewives, who adopted him as the son they wished were theirs. However, no evidence has come to light that his sequined renditions of Chopin inspired fans to discover the even greater pianistic gifts of Artur Rubinstein, a fellow son of Poland. The sleekly effusive performer may be fun, but he's also cultural dead-end kitsch.

Mae West's expert parodying of *femmes fatales,* in some of the campiest films of the 1930s, carried her to fame and riches. But in a long-delayed return to the screen in *Myra Breckenridge* (1970), Mae came a cropper. For the only time in her career, she wound up as kitsch, saddled with tasteless single-entendre lines. Even Raquel Welch outclassed that movie.

Alice Cooper (né Vincent Furnier of Detroit, Mich.), a rock star of the 1970s, strives to shock uptight Establishment-types, if any, at his performances. Here, the grotesquely made-up pop-culture idol shivers the spine with "Dead Babies" a number in which he skewers a doll and waves it around ghoulishly. More a boogieman from a low-budget horror movie than the terrifying specter he aims for, Cooper epitomizes the rancid staleness of what was once the fresh and genuinely exciting rock-music scene.

In the 1920s, during women's first era of liberation, they got—along with bobbed hair, the vote, and rolled stockings—their own sex object, Rudolph Valentino. In *The Young Rajah* (1922), Valentino's physical charms were displayed in pearl ropes and a jeweled jockstrap. But however he dressed—as an Eastern potentate, an Arab chieftain, or as a matador—Valentino was always kitsch's favorite male sex-kitten.

CHAPTER 9

Rich Kitsch And Other Lifestyles

If you've got it, flaunt it. If you haven't, fake it

Victorians, in their eagerness for respectability, sought to avoid domestic scandal by keeping books by male and female writers on separate shelves. With like skittishness, they concealed from susceptible gaze vulgar objects such as chair "limbs" ("legs," even in reference to furniture, had carnal connotations) behind velvet ruffles or beaded-fringe skirts. A later generation, while they welcomed telephony, regarded the phone itself as an interloper among the Nice Things about the house. They spared their sensibilities by hiding the naked instrument in a cabinet, or by secreting it beneath a cozy in the form of a proper lady in a long, crocheted gown.

Although fashions change, that muddling of self and possessions leads to the fragmenting of a coherent reality into a series of "images," a succession of new Me's. In pursuit of the chimera of Being With It, the shedding of ourselves like expendable snakeskins results in a kind of charade kitsch. Today, young people and those who would be youthful, bent on rejecting an uptight establishment, flock to "head" shops where they find clothing and accessories that proclaim the wearers as letting it all hang out. Mistaking lifestyle for life, they imagine that by arraying themselves in denim work clothes (time-savingly prefaded and artfully patched) they're participating in a more real world. Either unable or unwilling to see themselves as the mirror image of those they scorn, they're nevertheless painted with the brush of pretentious kitsch. Making a fetish of being Nobody, they parade their ponchos and dungarees at the opera and the theater in an inverse display of what Thorstein Veblen, an American social philosopher, called "conspicuous consumption."

Whether one indulges himself in the illusion that "Beautiful Things Make Beautiful People," as a chain of poverty-chic boutiques claims, or in the equally dubious fantasy that ritualistic spurning of the establishment endows us with a more authentic identity, the result is alienation kitsch, the outlandish search for oneself in externals. Only half aware of his Humpty Dumpty state, the new American seeks to get himself together through constant titillation from things outside himself. Thus, he attempts to rouse— or "raise," to use kitsch formulation—his consciousness through ingesting hallucinogens, getting into his horoscope, or battering his senses with the din of a portable radio, at work and at play.

A corollary of those frantic attempts to compel the external world to define him is the individual's flamboyant efforts to make a visible impact on the world. Visible, but in true kitsch fashion, not substantive. One such ineffectual assertion of the self is graffiti. Much of that glaringly colored advertisement for oneself consists, paradoxically, of anonymous nicknames that emit a muffled scream for recognition.

Bathtowels, highball glasses, or bedspreads bearing fake coats-of-arms and the owner's name are the passive middle-class counterpart of graffiti. Only in America, perhaps, can one acquire a synthetic self by buying a plastic, imitation stag's head "mounted on a walnut-finish plaque and with a full rack of elegant antlers and soft brown eyes, that adds warmth and outdoor charm to every den, family room, or bedroom." No matter that the proud city dweller hasn't hunted a day in his life; the trophy itself is a wish-fulfillment. It's like buying and showing off snapshots of someone else's summer vacation. Faced with the choice for his own vacation of viewing the natural sights of New Jersey or taking a trip to Africa, he instinctively opts for the least of both—a "safari" in an air-conditioned car to synthetic Jungle Habitat, crammed with wild animals incongruously set down in New Jersey. Thus, he sees neither New Jersey nor Africa.

For the very rich, the possibilities of kitsch identities are as unlimited as their purses will allow. In their heyday, American tycoons bought titled husbands for their daughters the way they bought racehorses and railroads for themselves. Their crowns of respectability did not come cheap. At the beginning of this century, the Goulds spent $5.5 million on a spendthrift French count, only to trade up a few years later for his cousin, the Duc de Talleyrand. The coming of the income tax changed the fashion from French and British noblemen to less expensive Polish princes, who, like custom-built foreign cars, soon became favored status symbols for Hollywood actresses.

Today, dream selves are mass-produced. For a mere $3,500, the affluent who have been long in city pent can own a make-believe ranch made of clear acrylic, complete with corrals, barns, cactuses, pastures, and silver-plated tweezers to hold down the livestock for branding in ink. In fact, the spread has all the accoutrements necessary to raising its herd of—mice.

The mouse-ranch syndrome is indicative of the kitsch that results from 20th-century man's divorce from his work. Obsessed by the desire to avoid labor, he clutters his life with instant devices, and spends the time he saves on do-it-yourself make-work. In that schizophrenic pursuit of meaningful accomplishment, he buys can't-miss kits, in which everything is precut and premeasured, for fashioning leather belts, decorative wall plaques, decoupage. It isn't just knickknacks he creates, but an image of life without failure.

Another example of the importance that rituals of success assume is the development of fail-safe cake mixes. When those prepackaged mixes first appeared on the market, they required only the addition of water. Surprisingly, they didn't sell. Not until they required the cook to add eggs did the mixes fulfill expectations. In adding a substantive ingredient, consumers could pretend that they were baking "homemade" cakes.

Having defeated the self-satisfaction, together with the burden, of work, the kitsch pursuit of leisure leads us as well to abort our pleasures. For example, mistaking the choosing, erecting, and decorating of a Christmas tree for time-consuming drudgery, we buy a uniformly and perfectly shaped tree of "natural vinyl," preassembled and, for a little more money, even pre-decorated. That such a festive ornament expresses nothing of ourselves and is identical to the one others have bought escapes our notice. But the void and the unconscious sense of nonentity that gnaws us as a result drive us to fantasy lives and kitsch exoticism.

Caught in a bland, automatized world, largely of his own making, the faceless man becomes a prey to Perk Up Kitsch. Ours has become an Age of Sensation, as we're exhorted to Cheer Up the living room, Liven Up last night's leftovers, and Pep Up our lives. Finding little satisfaction in the inconclusive problems of real life, and our inability to communicate with other people, we immerse ourselves in soap-opera heroines' courage and endless articulation of their innermost thoughts, and share at second hand the exploits of brain surgeons, private eyes, and lawyers who triumph decisively once a week. Such vicarious participation in excitement, evoking in us what Leslie Fiedler, an American literary critic and defender of mass taste, praises as "ecstasy," has fed the kitsch appetite for make-believe since the days of Horatio Alger, Jr.

When the reality of life becomes standardized, the hunger for variety impels us into a mania for kitsch exoticism. For example, foods must be taste thrills, an escape into strange and wonderful worlds of "gourmet" popcorn, chocolate-covered ants, or fried grasshoppers. To spur the imagination to believe that our lives have taken flight into rarefied realms, we devour the same, familiar frozen vegetables jumbled together and labeled variously as Italian, Hawaiian, Danish, French, and Japanese. The masquerading of kitsch exoticism as gourmet cooking reaches its apogee in the incongruity of burying subtly flavored foods, most notably bread, under a slathering of garlic butter.

As modern man has sensed increasingly his lack of communication with his fellow man, and his own dwindling powers of response despite his monosodium glutamate-drenched existence, he indulges more and more in what has been called "the new nonsense." Despairing of meaningful human contact, he fantasizes visitors from outer space who confide great truths to him, or endows to excess animals with human attributes.

He adorns his garden with coy kitsch signs reading "Chipmunk Crossing" or "Don't Look—Birds Bathing." He sees himself reflected in his pets. In a misguided attempt to be his dog's best friend, he encumbers the animal with all the paraphernalia that he lavishes on himself. Such dogged pursuit of petty kitsch includes mink coats, rhinestone collars, earrings, false eyelashes, and nail polish; Santa Claus, Halloween, and cowboy outfits; high chairs for "watching TV or sitting with the family"; portable car seats in zebra and leopard skin; haberdashery such as golf caps or yarmulkes bearing the Star of David.

To the kitsch-obsessed owner, a dog's house should be his castle, complete with cardboard battlements, wall-to-wall carpeting, and a sundeck. For the ultimate in beastly taste, an emporium in New York City sells doggy picnic bags with a choice of chicken chow mein, beef bourguignon, or steak-and-kidney pie, and two "pupcakes" with ice cream (kosher diets on request). Recently, sixty-five canine survivors of an American oil heiress woke one morning to find themselves sharing a bequest of $14 million and a 180-acre spread in Florida.

When all that disorientation of the hapless pet has taken its predictable toll, psychiatric help is available, for both animal and owner. As a reward for playing out others' fantasy roles, the Adored One may find its last repose in an elaborately marked grave at the Los Angeles Pet Cemetery. But not until religious services are over.

Kitsch is an imitation of life, a masquerade in which we don disguises to fool ourselves. We put our hands over our eyes and ask, "Guess who?"

Even the television industry scrambles aboard the poverty-chic denim bandwagon with a precision electronics instrument wrapped in the rugged material. For a touch of contemporary elegance, sew on embroidered patches.

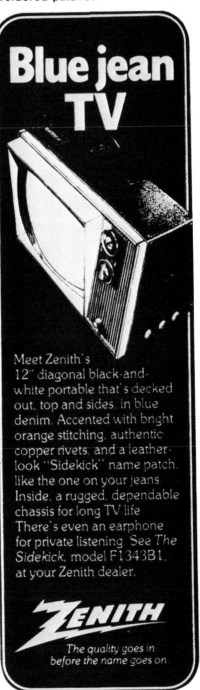

Blue jeans have traveled a long way from Idaho potato farms. Today, those work pants have become status symbols, with their embroidered patches, the more of them the jazzier. Jeans freaks and the Beautiful People pay up to $500 for a "personalized," hand-sewn pair. This young man typifies kitsch's inability to let well enough alone, as he adds more and more kitsch glamor to his dungarees.

Terribly chic. Kitsch finally blurs all distinctions between values, so that drug addiction and euphoric flights become "alternate lifestyles." Even further removed from reality are these kitsch icons—an image-creating T-shirt and a plastic marijuana plant that permit fantasies of a fantasy existence.

Thrill on thrill for boredom-ridden lives. With a poster depicting couples entwined in sexual acts, an herbalist plays medicine man in his astrology shop.

What the Vanderbilts wanted, the Vanderbilts got. When Mrs. William K. (later Mrs. O.H.P. Belmont, famous for her advice to a fellow suffragette, "Pray to God. She will help you") Vanderbilt decided to buy a titled husband for her daughter, Consuelo (1877-1964), nobody would do but the Duke of Marlborough. The most beautiful of the bartered brides, Consuelo pleaded in vain, but not even her tearful refusal on the day of the wedding, in 1895, prevented her parents from getting the duke they'd paid for. Here she stands in her robes for the coronation of Edward VII.

Be a world-traveler without leaving home. Try upgrading your life by slapping these genuine hotel stickers on your luggage. Be careful, though; some of the hotels haven't been known by these names for years.

From her birth in an opera box in Keokuk, Iowa, through careers as a pianist in a nickelodeon, a columnist, a lecturer, and the author of several volumes of autobiography, Elsa Maxwell (1883-1963) reached her pinnacle of success as a hired party-thrower for the world's notables. Despite well-publicized feuds with luminaries, from the Duchess of Windsor to Elvis Presley, Miss Maxwell through nearly five decades radiated an unremitting gaiety. Her genius for splashy entertaining found its completest expression in the fantastic fancy-dress balls she staged for the very rich, in New York, London, Paris, Cannes, Venice —wherever the international set congregated. This photograph shows the costumed mistress of revels in an uncharacteristic moment of repose.

Homemaker kitsch mistrusts the merely ornamental as impractical; it respects the useful, but insists on a decorative appeal and a conventional lifestyle. Even scruffy, strung-out hippie layabouts, if subdued and scrubbed, may attain the revered status of the American eagle, Dürer's *Hands of an Apostle,* and baby's discarded booties by becoming bookends. (7″)

Conspicuous consumption among New York's horsy set, 1903-style. Festoons of electric lights and a cyclorama depicting an imaginary landscape adorned C.K.G. Billings's famed dinner party for his friends at Sherry's restaurant. Each guest sat in splendor at his own table. (The horses had already eaten.)

15380

Some affluent couples don't have to walk a mile for their camels. Instead, they order a now-you-have-everything pair of beasts from a Neiman-Marcus catalog, that fabulous wish-book emanating annually from the opulent store in Dallas, Texas. Delivery time, the ordering directions point out, is subject to availability of camels, which will be flown to your "private oasis" anywhere within the continental U.S. For those setting out on the final journey, the store offered genuine his-and-hers mummy cases.

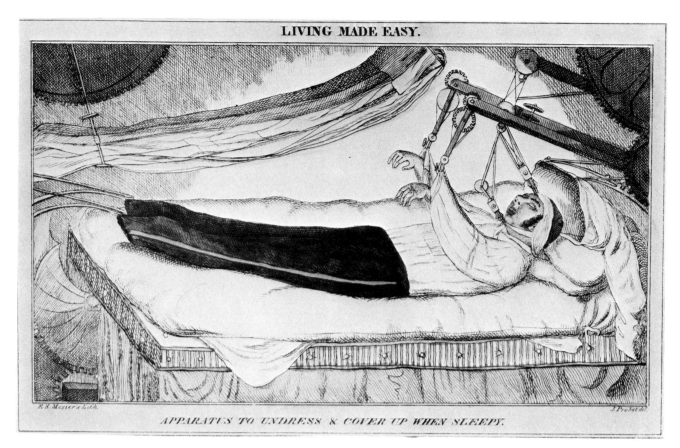

APPARATUS TO UNDRESS & COVER UP WHEN SLEEPY.

Alexis de Tocqueville was not the only prophet of kitsch. Robert Seymour's series of twelve lithographs, *Living Made Easy: Dedicated to the Utilitarian Society,* satirized a gadget-dominated existence. Published in New York in 1832, they anticipated automated kitsch life, in which we are the object, and the machine is the active participant. (9¾"x6")

One way to throw your opponent off his game is to pull out this putter in the shape of a human foot. Yet another instant-laugh fix for jaded lives.

143

Preparing crackers a certain way can produce a mock-apple pie. In this muffin mix, apples substitute for blueberries. So far, no one has come up with a cracker made from blueberry flour; but kitsch ingenuity will find a way.

The Top Layer

The top layer in a barrel of apples is generally the best in the barrel. The "top layer" is always the best in everything—except in a

SHREDDED WHEAT BISCUIT

Desperately overreaching for a touch of class, the National Biscuit Company proposed to our grandparents a rich sauce of creamed oysters poured over a shredded wheat biscuit. The silver service was intended to raise the gustatorial tone of the ambitious dish. Luckily, a plain portion of the breakfast food stands by—just in case.

Only a sample of the clever touch you can give your Great American Meals parties. Hearty Western franks 'n' beans call for the Conestoga wagon salt 'n' pepper set. Having a chowder 'n' chat get together? Your dining room becomes a friendly general store, complete with a rockin'-chairs-'n'-cracker-barrels atmosphere, with the pair of potbelly stoves. 'N' Mason jars are just right for your next turkey 'n' all the fixin's feast. When meals have lost their savor, kitsch prompts us to cuteness. (2¾", 4", 3¼")

Red and white and cobalt blue—
Bombs are fun and tasty, too.

There will always be customers who fall for the snobbery of the "for a few pennies more" kitsch pitch. Even for popcorn.

Horatio Alger, Jr. (1834-99) wrote more than a hundred inspirational novels for boys, demonstrating that for likely lads who make the most of their chances, wealth and happiness will surely follow. Blessed with unnatural goodness, Alger's smug, mannerly heroes—Tattered Tom and Ragged Dick, for example—were exaggerated embodiments of the Reverend Russell H. Conwell's "Acres of Diamonds" philosophy that the pathway to riches begins in one's own backyard.

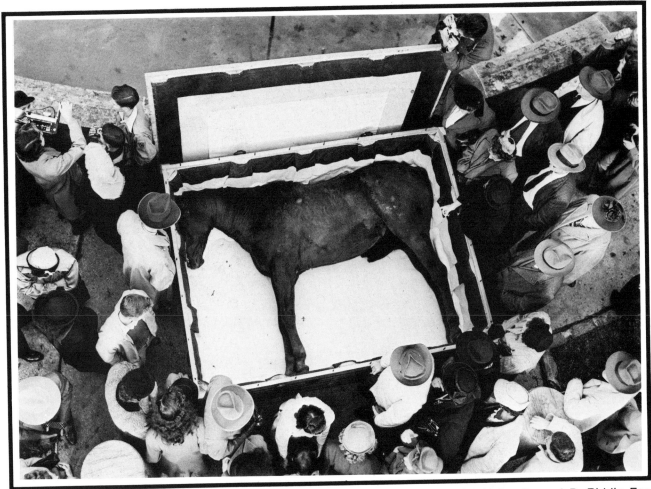

Man-o-War, the most famous American racehorse, succumbed to a heart attack in 1947. He had earned for his owner a million dollars in prize money, stud fees, and by the sale of his foals. At the Samuel D. Riddle Faraway Farms, near Lexington, Kentucky, the noble steed lies in state in a Brobdingnagian travesty of a casket.

Pets at rest. A doghouse mausoleum and a master's ashes buried with the remains of his dogs are but two of the sights at the Hartsdale (New York) Canine Cemetery. Greater love hath no pet lover, nor greater alienation from his own humanity.

Genre painting at its most heart-warmingly kitschy. Reproductions of the oil paintings portraying poker-playing pooches that Cassius M. Coolidge, a New York City artist, did early in this century are still available in shops and by mail. *His Station and Four Aces,* like others in the series, is "ideal for bar, den, card or rumpus room, finished in an oil effect." (14"x9½")

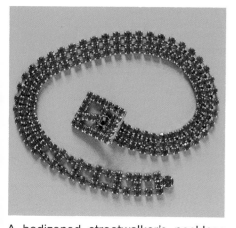

A bedizened streetwalker's necklace of simulated gold and jewels. This dog collar is the final word in transference of kitsch striving for grandeur. What pet owners see reflected in all those rose-colored fragments is themselves.

The domestic life of the Borden Company's Elsie the Cow was always a kitsch-coy reflection of American stereotypes. The bovine house-wife was never more arch than in this equating of cows' "giving their all" with World War II soldiers' giving their lives in defense of their country.

Two hundred years of American independence. I'll drink to that! The bell that rang out the momentous news in 1776, and which over half a century later cracked while tolling for the death of Chief Justice John Marshall, becomes just another set of stacked coasters. The red-white-and-blue bow makes the Liberty Bell authentically patriotic. (6")

Establishment-rejection kitsch reaches a climax of sorts in the T-shirt shown at the far right of this New York head-shop window.

Pure linen damask, fine china, and solid gold flatware—surely there's nothing kitsch here. However, the cloth is washable plastic and the china is a garish transfer-printed miniaturization of pseudo-Fragonard elegance. Gold cutlery is, this side of the court of the Medicis, vulgarly ostentatious. Silver, plated to look like gold, is even kitschier. The stainless steel shown here, gold-washed to look like gold-plated silver, is pitiful. All that is missing from this dinner table is a pair of butane-burning, eternal candles.

Anthropomorphism at one of its dizziest and kitschiest heights. What makes this gag newsphoto especially repellent is that the basking woman appears quite content to hold hands with a monkey.

The "colorful, practical, hygienic, and roomy" Kitty Cottage is just the thing for a cat with hang-ups about being observed "when nature calls." The cute-kitsch label on the half-timbered hideaway hammers home the point: Kitty A [sic] Go Go.

"Monkeys is the cwaziest people," the zany comic Lew Lehr used to say. But not so silly as those who found amusing Lawson Wood's popular and kitschy illustrations of humanoid monkeys. The mother's hair style and the gratuitous presence of a watermelon inject sly and cruel racist overtones into this "Look, they're almost human" inanity.

Hugh Hefner provides scampering visions of solace for bachelors at heart. This bevy of bunnies dispense cheer and viands at the many Playboy Clubs scattered about the biggest American cities. In an age when pets have become more human than people, what more fitting than that people should be seen as pet rabbits, cute little sex machines?

Flower children of yesteryear. What the artist had in mind when he drew the picture for this unpleasant postcard is anyone's guess. Children at play—but what's the game in which a butterfly-child receives a battering from one companion and an arrow in his head from another playmate? *Kinderkitsch.*

This 1964 postage stamp celebrated U.S. Homemakers. It forsook the reality of mid 20th-century life in favor of a sentimental sampler depicting a greeting card idyll.

150

If you're anxious for to shine, wear this plastic corsage with a light bulb in the center. Kitsch outshines nature. (5½")

Dedicated lovers of kitsch don't settle for two-levered nutcrackers, unless they're shaped like women's legs. They don't even expect you to mistake these specimens for a real cider press or an anvil. But you're going to notice them. (12", 4")

Vinous Rubber Grapes

Patented U. S. of America, Nov. 17, 1887. Also in England and France

For Theatre Goers
THESE GOODS ARE PUT UP IN OPERA GLASS CASES.

(MUSCATEL)

For Sleighing Parties
These Goods are put up in Opera Glass Cases, neatly suspended around the neck.

Also put up with RYE, ROCK AND GINGER.

Brandy   Gin   Whiskey
Port   Sherry   Madeira   Muscat

Ingenious, but repulsive, kitsch. In 1887, a Philadelphia firm came up with a discreet way for theater-goers to have a few nips *between* intermissions, while pretending to reach for their opera glasses. According to the manufacturer, its "Vinous Rubber Grapes are pure rubber capsules filled and expanded to the capacity of a small pony glassful of fifteen grapes or drinks of either Whisky, Brandy or Gin, or eighteen smaller grapes filled with the most popular wines . . . When putting in the mouth, press the lips tightly together, bend the head forward slightly, then crush the grape between the teeth, or insert a pin or toothpick between the lips and penetrate the grape. After swallowing the contents eject the skin."

The drunk has always been a subject for comedy, holding up to laughter man's foibles and lack of good sense. Kitsch asks us to see alcoholism, whether real or simulated, as manly, clever, and dazzlingly sophisticated. Here, Dean ("Dino") Martin, a popular entertainment personality who works supposed dipsomania into his comedy routines, promotes his own brand of liquor.

A battery-powered liquor decanter for the Embassy reception or the Board of Directors meeting, or for an impeccably staged revival of Nöel Coward's play *Design for Living.* Press a button, and the obliging tyke "urinates" into your glass. (13")

There's a sucker for "something different" born every minute. A perennial favorite with mail-order house customers, specially designed ice-cube trays turn out "bountifully proportioned beauties guaranteed to give nippy delight." Despite the curves of the "cool cuties," the idea is foursquare, oral erotic kitsch.

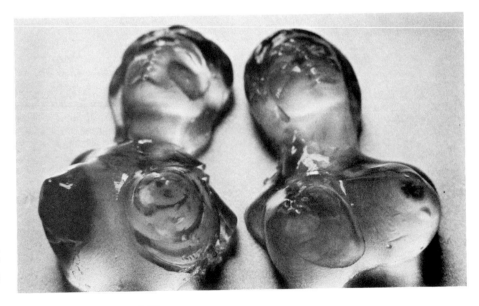

From The Cradle To The Grave

A tacky world of birth, sex, marriage, and death

The wedding ceremony is over, but all is not lost. Photos and a taped recording of the "I do's," combined in a music-box album rigged to tinkle "I Love You Truly" when the cover is raised, will in years to come restore luster to dimmed memories of the nuptials. Have you chosen the best possible place to spend your honeymoon—alone together, where Something Wonderful is guaranteed to happen? . . .

In the drag race of sexual competency, the old engine begins wheezing and sputtering just as you're entering the win-or-lose hairpin turn marked "Final Stretch: You're Thirty Years Old." Your battery is giving out on you when you need it most. Are you heading back, limping and lurching, to the pits, with the other losers? . . .

There's already enough clutter around the house, and you're tempted to dispose of Baby's first shoes. But throwing away those adorable booties is almost as unthinkable as tossing out Baby. The Muse of Kitsch, heeding your anguished cry for guidance, inspires you with a solution. Keep those artifacts of fleeting infancy and, at the same time, put them to work. Transform the shoes into cherished heirlooms as a lamp base or book ends; or display them annually with the balls and tinsel on the Christmas tree. However, you don't want them bronzed; that's corny. What to do? . . .

Out in the garden, you hear the telephone ring while you're cutting roses for the dining-room table. You learn that an aunt and uncle, a few miles away, have succumbed to flu. Ignoring the perfectly beautiful fresh flowers in the garden, you consult the Yellow Pages for the name of a florist from whom you order, sight unseen, a spray of too-perfectly beautiful hothouse flowers. . . .

As the world was for Wordsworth, kitsch is so much with us that we're unaware of its pervasiveness in our cradle-to-grave customs. It diverts us from personally directed observance of private matters and occasions toward complex or blatant exhibitionism. Hokily pretentious rituals celebrating birth, sexual experience, marriage, and death have become vulgar tokens of the simple, the direct, and the spontaneous. Catering to today's obsession with sexual liberation, slick magazines such as *Viva*, *Playboy*, and *Playgirl* overflow with ads for sex manuals: "What to do . . . How to do it . . . When to do it . . . Over 750 actual photographs show you, step by step, all you will ever need to know to satisfy completely your love partner." Those magazines, and the books they advertise, see sexual technique and sexual satisfaction not as a thing apart, but as man and woman's whole existence.

If the overblown promises of kitsch in the illustrated sex guides remain unfulfilled; if skilled applications of vaginal lubricants, available in a mouth-watering array of flavors from strawberry to champagne, fail to turn on at least one of the participants; if one or more of the seemingly infinite variety of dildos or simulated body orifices disappoints; if chains, whips, thongs, or hot-wax drippings don't fill the bill, then perhaps getting oneself up in Frederick's of Hollywood underwear for women and men—all peekaboo nipples and titillating tumescence—will arouse the weakened flesh. The horny loner can buy a pair of life-size inflatable plastic dolls ("Your own personal slaves of pleasure") and observe, or pretend to observe, their carryings-on. Such His and Hers surrogate sex personae, perhaps the ultimate in kitsch sex, represent the perfect "successful sex" formula, a pure fantasy with no chance of failure.

In this age of sensationalism, the urge to make Those Special Moments stand out from run-of-the-mill sensational moments propels us into kitsch's waiting arms. Weddings on fire engines; in diver's gear, underwater; on roller coasters; or in the nude, are exhibitionistic travesties of the personal touch so ardently pursued today. For those who are diffident and desirous of a fairyland wedding, there stands ready for hire the kitsch palace, a mélange of Hollywood-prop, Colonial-Sicilian-Oriental elegance. The blowout reception, in the hands of a professional director, features a Ziegfeldian wedding cake enclosing an electric-powered fountain. On top are a plastic bride and groom, beneath whom coyly lurks a naked, newborn babe.

The honeymooning couple, instead of going on a private trip, can join a flock-in with other newlyweds at elaborate rural retreats, dotted with individual "chalets," where Something Wonderful happens amid surroundings that include a heart-shaped canopy bed and a heart-shaped sunken tub, encircled provocatively with floor-to-ceiling mirrors. To add to the snapshots and tapes of the wedding ceremony, an automatic camera will take color movies of bathtub cavortings. In short, the entire prepackaged event is a snickering evocation of dawn-to-dawn sex in an environment that would delight a "belle époque" madam.

Bronzed booties may be old shoe to mildly afflicted fetishists, but recent strides in the baby-shoe preservation industry are encouraging. Baby's shoes can now be porcelainized and painted plain or fancy—just like fine dinner china. The ceramic artifacts can survive as table or bookshelf ornaments or as paperweights to remind us that obstreperous teenagers were once biddable babes. For a more public display of parental pride, shoes make a diverting change from shrunken heads or outsize dice hung from the rear-view mirror of the family car. What tribal change accounts for the substitution of infants' footwear for the kitsch favorite of yesteryear, the upturn-bottomed baby posed on a bearskin, may fascinate anthropologists of the future.

Nothing so reveals the artificializing of once deep, private feelings as the American way of death, the final kitsch spectacular. With rouged face and tinted hair, the corpse, dressed for an eternal beddy-byes, lies on a satin-sheeted bed in a "slumber room." What were once personal tributes have become standardized floral arrangements of waxen, hothouse perfection. Imagine the consternation today if friends arrived at a funeral with a bouquet picked from their own garden. Someday, somebody is bound to think of a coordinated color scheme registered at the local florist, like a bride's silverware pattern. Grieving friends' carrying the coffin and lowering it into the grave have given way to effortlessly rolling dollies and push-button elevators. And atop the grave, not a strewing of fragile blossoms, bespeaking the sweetness and brevity of life, but a showy, false, and parodistic spray of plastic flowers.

O kitsch, where is thy victory?

What every couple—married or otherwise—already knows is turned into an arcane art. Lyrical hints at exotic naughtiness engender the fear that most people, lacking expertise, are doing it all wrong. Kitsch, pursuing its mechanical, take-as-directed promises, tries to go successful marriage one better by confusing supersex with perfect happiness.

Mail-order catalogs and far-out magazines advertise these battery-powered Magic Massage Wands, whose "gentle, deep penetrating action rubs away foot cramps, takes the kink out of sore muscles. Tuck it in your handbag, keep it in your office desk for on-the-spot relief." Anyone who believes that sales pitch will believe anything. The surrogate penis costs from three to twelve dollars, and comes in "flesh-colored" or "black" in sizes ranging from four to twelve inches.

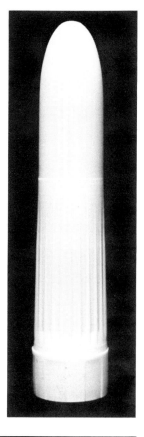

This vinyl sex mate makes not only "all other dolls obsolete" but, ostensibly, real women as well.

Another, more elaborate and expensive version of the woman's home companion.

NEW BRITAIN, CONN., Sept. 7, 1969—Newlyweds "Krunch" and "Mamma Robin" rode the groom's flower-bedecked motorcycle through an aisle formed by the bikes of their fellow Drifters Motorcycle Club members following an outdoor ceremony in A.W. Stanley Park yesterday. The bride, who wore a simple white ankle-length gown and a veil of white tulle, and the groom, dressed in dungarees and black leather, set off by silver chains, exchanged vows while seated on the cycle. After the ceremony, the couple za-roomed off on their honeymoon as the congregation revved its congratulations.

Tiny Tim achieved brief fame for his falsetto-voiced rendition of "Tip-Toe Thru the Tulips With Me." In 1969, he exploited his marriage to "Miss Vickie" by turning it into an entertainment "special" on Johnny Carson's nationally televised "Tonight Show."

Lottie Howard
"Mrs. Living Corpse"
BURIED ALIVE!
Thursday June 9, 1966

More wedding kitschuals. At a drive-in theater in Denison, Texas, a groom took an underground wife after she had been "buried" for a week. In 1967, a couple, together with their nine attendants, donned rubber formal wedding gear for the "big plunge" to the bottom of a giant fish tank. In a wedding of painted dolls, in San Francisco in 1971, a real-life Raggedy Ann and Andy vowed to play house till death do them part.

The sacredness of marriage vows is somewhat at variance with quickie-marriage factories such as this one at Salome, Arizona.

Weddings are favorite occasions for the kitschy display of wealth, either real or assumed. In these purse-proud productions, like the one depicted in the film *Goodbye, Columbus* (1969), the bride and groom play decidedly secondary rôles. The real stars are the bride's parents, the begetters of the fabulous wedding feast.

Hardly the wedding-cake ornament to delight the Women's Liberation movement. It's the old story of the man-hungry harpy snaring a reluctant male. (7½")

Let 'em eat kitsch. This M-G-M musical production of a wedding cake is designed primarily to feast eyes upon A-budget extras, including a motorized fountain.

Pure as the driven snow—99⁴⁴/₁₀₀ percent worth. The soap, that is. Marilyn Chambers displays tokens of her double-barreled fame as the Ivory Snow ad model and as an actress of phenomenal capability in *Behind the Green Door*, 1973's notorious porno flick.

This joylessly conceived stork looks more as if it were about to devour the infant than deliver it to a happy household. Postcard humor can sometimes have a bizarre edge to it, as this turn-of-the-century example attests.

Get me to the church in time! For those who didn't and are now "radiantly pregnant," it's a "big new look" in wedding fashions. The headpiece is tied, "harem style," with a string of pearls. The pregnancy-chic gown is incongruously white.

Too cute for words. Angel babies, with bottoms lifted; mint-filled prams; storks and nesting hens—plastic offerings to launch baby on a plastic existence.

To the unwary eye, this sentimental Valentine's Day remembrance might seem to be simply schlock. However, this particular item passes from schlock to kitsch. When the box is opened, a palpitating red heart chatters its ghoulishly literal message.

Offbeat sexual innuendoes were a staple of Hollywood movies before they became absolutely explicit. In *Tarzan, the Ape Man* (1932), learning to count takes on a decided air of foot fetishism.

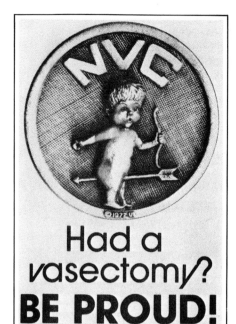

Had a *vasectomy?*
BE PROUD!

Join the National Vasectomy Club and let the world know you feel great about yourself. One dollar entitles you to membership and a bumper sticker. Another $5.95, and you get a fun conversation piece... NVC's emblem in silver to wear as tie tac or lapel pin. Mail

Only the most compulsive joiners and exhibitionists would wear this ridiculous kitsch badge. Cupid has shot his last bolt and castrated himself in this unpleasantly inaccurate emblem of vasectomy.

Screw you.
It's the thought that counts.

We sell it in 14kt. gold and sterling silver. We also say "love" and a

Kitsch lays it on the line.

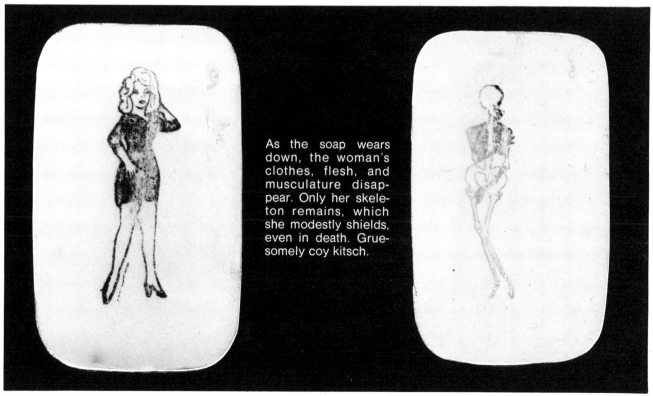

As the soap wears down, the woman's clothes, flesh, and musculature disappear. Only her skeleton remains, which she modestly shields, even in death. Gruesomely coy kitsch.

Showman Florenz Ziegfeld (William Powell in *Ziegfeld Follies,* 1946) awaits the eternal companionship of his wife, Billie Burke. Here is Hollywood's view of heaven, complete with silk pajamas, electrified candelabra, and workday and Sunday-best wings hanging in the closet. Apparently, the film industry's prohibition of double beds did not extend into the hereafter.

Kitschy mordant humor assails the passerby of this cemetery, near Chicago.

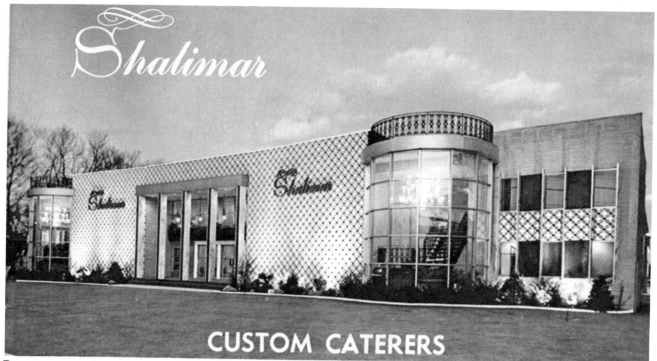

Shalimar

CUSTOM CATERERS

Baroque crystal chandeliers combine with cement block and gold-anodized aluminum, real and plastic shrubbery, and a statue of Buddha. In short, an all-purpose wedding or bar mitzvah palazzo, in New York City.

Honeymoon hideaways feature bathtubs that would rouse the most jaded Roman emperor to envy. A resort nestled in the Pocono Mountains of Pennsylvania features an automatic movie camera that records the post-nuptial frolics for hard-core home entertainment. If all this stimulation is required to add spice to a honeymoon, what will a couple need to maintain their enthusiasm in the years to come?

Personalized-porcelainized baby shoes have replaced bronzed or copper-plated ones. One baby-step forward for mankind.

The laugh in this visual pun, so proudly emblazoned on the jockey shorts, is on the wearer. The would-be sign of virility is less a lusty "Cock-a-doodle-doo!" than a frisky Chicken Little.

A foam-rubber bathmat to tickle the feet and the fancy of sadistic bachelors. (14"x13")

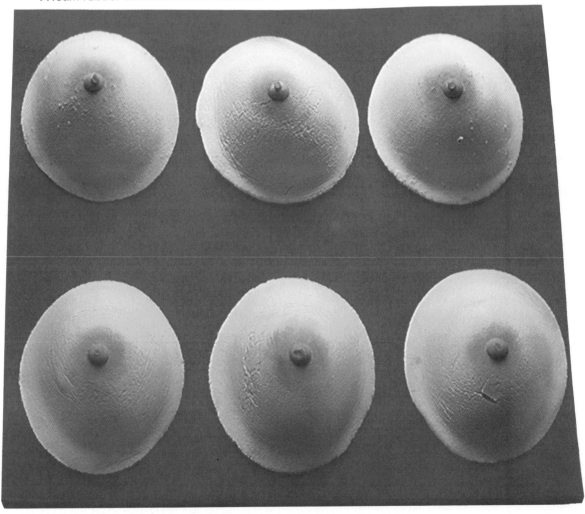

Victorian verities abound in Green-Wood Cemetery, in Brooklyn, New York. Master Rosekrans's stone, with its tiny cloak and single empty shoe, typifies the maudlin sentimentality of that era. Upon a grander monument, the Lawsons face eternity in self-satisfied domesticity, their well-fed and well-clothed earthliness at distracting variance with the incorporeal timelessness of heaven. The pompously rotund Mr. Wood, *(overleaf)* striking an oratorical attitude atop his castle, seems to say, like Shelley's Ozymandias, "Look on my works, ye Mighty, and despair!"

Merchandising of death. This brochure promotes a pretense of perpetual individuality through gravestones (always called "monuments" in the trade). The reality is to be seen at Calvary Cemetery in Long Island City, New York, burial ground for over two million "individuals." On the horizon of that necropolis rises, not the tombstones of Titans, but the skyline of Manhattan.

What Is A Monument

 MONUMENT IS FAR MORE THAN A MEANS OF MARKING THE RESTING PLACE OF AN INDIVIDUAL OR A FAMILY.

IT IS A SYMBOL OF DEVOTION. IT IS A TANGIBLE EXPRESSION OF THE NOBLEST OF ALL HUMAN EMOTIONS — *LOVE*.

IT SHOULD NOT REFLECT SORROW BUT RATHER THE LONG YEARS OF WARMTH AND AFFECTION TYPICAL OF THE AMERICAN FAMILY.

A MONUMENT IS BUILT BECAUSE THERE WAS A LIFE — NOT A DEATH; AND WITH INTELLIGENT SELECTION AND PROPER GUIDANCE SHOULD INSPIRE REVERENCE, FAITH AND HOPE FOR THE LIVING.

AS AN ESSENTIAL PART OF OUR AMERICAN WAY OF LIFE, A MONUMENT SHOULD SPEAK OUT AS A VOICE FROM YESTERDAY AND TODAY TO AGES YET UNBORN —

Typing Exercises

A key to racist, ethnic, and sexist kitsch

The diminutive hero of *Little Nemo in Slumberland*, Winsor McCay's classic American comic strip of seventy years ago, preferred dream kingdoms to his drab waking world. Like Nemo, kitsch racists and sexists value soothing and self-aggrandizing make-believe over disturbing reality. One of the most effective ways that man has devised to protect his superhero self-image is to disparage those who, he imagines, are not complete human beings, let alone fellow-superheroes. Thus, the pecking order of an Orwellian animal farm reduces the "enemy"—whether it's the Yellow Peril, the Black Menace, or the Little Woman—who threatens invasion of social and business preserves, to inept and idiotic figures of fun or condescending contempt.

Just as kitsch assumes that there's always room at the top for the grand and the splendid in the arts (and produces instead the merely grandiose and splendiferous), so the kitsch attitude toward imposed inferior status adopts the comfortable, if false, notion that the butts of our own bigotry are conveniently gathered in the social structure's cellar for the purpose of being society's resident Big Jokes or Big Threats. In their assigned role as comic figures, blacks have been depicted as superstitious, watermelon-gorging, gin-swilling, dancing simpletons. More recently, they've been cast either as dangerous conspirators in a militant revolution or as Cadillac-charioted pimps and pushers. Even Mark Twain, the creator of Jim, Huck Finn's heroic friend and mentor, could say that "the Yellow Terror is threatening this world today. It is looming vast and ominous."

To males who feel their "superiority" endangered by females, women are finger-nibbling ninnies who, like "sweet Alice" in *Ben Bolt*, a popular 19th-century American poem, should weep with delight at their masculine smile and tremble with fear at their frown. When cast in their Big Threat role, women become castrating viragos. Therefore, it's best to keep them busy at birthing and baking, and endearingly unbalancing the family checkbook. Or grant them their natural fulfillment as scorchingly passionate sex objects, fit only to parade a bosomy sexuality at automobile and boat shows, or in ads and television commercials hustling everything from flashlight batteries to office duplicating machines.

George Orwell observed of "classless" societies that everyone is equal, but some are more equal than others. Needing reassuring tokens of his success, the social climber addicts himself to the kitsch confusion of class with snobbery. Addressing himself to an invisible aristocracy of which he imagines that he's a part, he says, "We're better than the others." And so next to his easy chair, he places a painted wooden black man in livery holding an ashtray, and on a nearby table, a lamp in the form of a torch-bearing, turbaned blackamoor.

Kitsch, in many of its guises, is a facile assumption of the rightness of things. Nowhere is that more apparent than in racist kitsch and in male chauvinism. Kitsch condescension differs from racial hatred in that it's often obsessed with the sentimental notion that those in inferior positions enjoy their rôle. The banjo-strumming Uncle Tom, Hollywood's once-popular black maid whose sole happiness is doin' fo' the gorgeously gowned white quality who's *so* rich and pretty, and the television commercial wife whose life finds daily satisfaction in her husband's smiling approbation of a decently brewed pot of coffee are clearly content in that station to which it has pleased their mistress or master, if not God, to call them.

The objects of racist and sexist stereotypes, once they have been dehumanized, can be guiltlessly exploited for tasteless humor: a pottery black face, with popped eyes and smiling open mouth ready and willing to receive flicked cigarette ashes; a toilet-bowl swab, its handle made in the likeness of an obliging black mammy; a nutcracker waggishly in the form of a woman's shapely legs. All just good-natured fun, they pretend, but too insistently to be thoroughly convincing.

As the victims of the longest sustained discrimination, women and blacks have been the principal targets of the ugliest of all kinds of kitsch. But various ethnic minorities, in their turn, have felt its sting — Jews as hooked-nose, pushy moneylenders, Chinese as no-tickee no-shirtee launderers or as sinister white slavers and opium den overlords, the Irish as top-o'-the-mornin' cops or dumb housemaids. Present-day examples are relative rareties, eliminated, ironically, by the very social mobility that created them. As minority groups gain self-awareness, power to enforce their rights, and acceptance as equals, their kitsch exploitation dwindles into quaint echoes of the past. Already, offensive caricatures of blacks have disappeared from gift shops, movies, and advertising. Progress toward the liberation of women, of more recent origin, has had as yet less impact on sexist kitsch. The society pages of newspapers still picture almost exclusively women in marriage announcements. That one more female is off her parents' hands, has landed her man, and has made it to the altar, her rightful goal, is still occasion for tribal rejoicing.

Perhaps someday, racist and sexist kitsch items and attitudes will disappear. Almost none bedevil America's newest minority, the Puerto Ricans. A hopeful sign of a new awakening. But the urge to return to Slumberland with Little Nemo — "Oh, dear! I wish I could go to sleep again," secure from harsh realities and complexities — is a compelling opiate.

It is to trap dreams of taste, grandeur, position, a sense of belonging, of being with it, or above it all, that people lay the snare of kitsch. But the dreams always elude capture; kitsch mockingly hoists the trapper by his own petard.

These Currier and Ives commercial cards of 1880 heap ridicule on the recently freed "uppity" blacks. Some of them flaunt their absurdly garish clothes; others, like this arrogantly grinning road hog with his jug of corn liquor, snobbishly lord it over their betters.

SAY SAMBO, HO! WHERE IS YOUR SHOE?
THOSE CHEAP CUT NAILS WILL NEVER DO,
'TIS HARD TO BEAT A HORSE WELL SHOD,
WITH PUTNAM NAILS FORGED FROM THE ROD.

A feckless black is outdistanced in all respects by the white driver and his spanking horse. Advertising cards of the late 19th century, precursors of the picture postcard, were a popular medium for disparaging, racist humor.

A sudden rise in wool

The theme of this early 20th-century "comic" postcard is the legendary inborn fearfulness of blacks.

This caricature statuette of painted wood (5½") from the 1940s exemplifies Your Ideal Negro: a valet, beaming in happy anticipation of a chance to serve white folks.

Richard Felton Outcault (1863-1928) created some well-known comic strips, including "The Yellow Kid" (1896) and "Buster Brown" (1902). Another Outcault comic strip was "Pore Lil Mose," which ran in the New York *Herald,* 1901-2. The series constantly ridiculed its diminutive black hero (who left Cottonville, Georgia, to seek his fortune in New York) and his family. Their quaint language, antics, and thieving ways were pointed up in order to evoke derisive laughter in white folks, who of course knew how to speak and behave.

Kitsch often perceives the life of Afro-Americans as a state of childlike innocence and toe-tapping mirth. Nowhere is the double-cliché view more directly stated than in the song "All God's Chillun Got Rhythm," from *A Day at the Races* (1937), a Marx Brothers vehicle.

Stereotypes of blacks were constantly reinforced by the movies. Stepin Fetchit, seen here with Will Rogers in *Judge Priest* (1934), never wanted for employment so long as he played the shuffling and molasses-slow shirker. American audiences found Fetchit a perpetual source of fun, as they did Mantan Moreland, his contemporary, whose specialty was pop-eyed fright and the line, delivered on the run, "Feet, do yo' stuff!"

In a magazine advertisement of the 1880s, opera diva Adelina Patti attests that she got her lovely white skin by using Pears' soap. The black man, with a knowing wink, tries vainly to make the soap do as much for him. (How "complecksun" differs from "complexion" in pronunciation is a secret known only to kitsch dialecticians.)

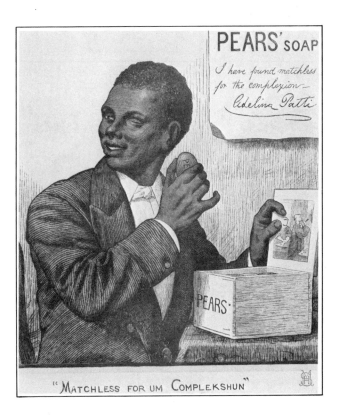

"MATCHLESS FOR UM COMPLEKSHUN"

The 1877 ad for Lautz soaps actually shows the scouring efficacy of their product: a black is made desirably white by its use. For the following century, skin bleaches and hair straighteners were a mark of induced self-loathing that had been instilled in blacks. In their attempt to gain social acceptance, they sought to obliterate their racial characteristics and become pseudo-whites.

During the recent wave of black exploitation films such as *Shaft's Big Score!* (1972), with Richard Roundtree, the newly liberated black male is reduced to Superstud, irresistible to all women (the simplistic kitsch view of racial equality), and elevated to Invincible Annihilator of his enemies. In short, one hokey dehumanization has replaced another.

For decades, the fear of Orientals was fed by racist fantasies. The terror of inundation by a Yellow Tide of cheap labor that would deprive native Americans of jobs was reinforced by imagined threats. This obviously faked photograph, of the early 20th century, purports to expose the enslaving of flowers of American womanhood by Chinese traffickers in opium.

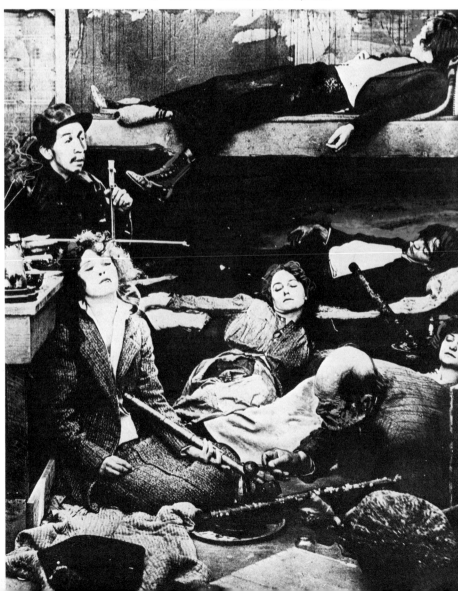

Ming the Merciless; or, The Yellow Peril. Caucasian actor Charles Middleton played the Oriental archfiend in *Flash Gordon,* the 1930s' film version of the popular comic strip. Myrna Loy and Boris Karloff showed us what the Yellow Menace was up to, in *The Mask of Fu Manchu* (1932).

I'M OUT FOR A GOOD TIME-AND-A-HALF

A MUTOSCOPE CARD   PRINTED IN U.

Pictorial puns raise otherwise routine girlie art to
the ranks of pin-up kitsch.

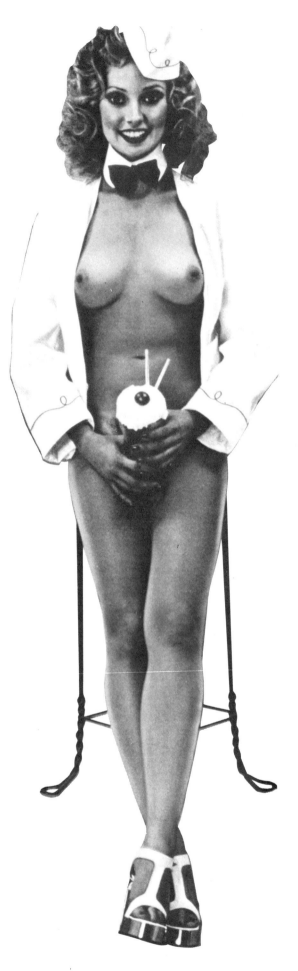

In these congratulatory cards, the female graduate is saluted as a cute satisfier of immediate needs; but the male is a serious person, someone with a long-range future.

An innocent greeting card, carried away by its exaggerated sentiment, stumbles into seeming like an advertisement for the widely popular, pornographic film *Deep Throat.*

A gallimaufry of kitsch fantasies crowd this scene from Cecil B. De-Mille's *Don't Change Your Husband* (1919). Gloria Swanson as a dominating sex goddess sits enthroned on an oiled trio of prostrate, virile Nubians, against a peculiar background of moire masonry. The desire to enslave blacks is made more piquant by the strong suggestion of taboo interracial sex.

◄ Waste not want not. A World War I government agency urges patriots to conserve paper and thus release poison gas on the enemy. And a few years earlier, a temperance postcard, with kitsch's typical doublethink, proposes genocide as a way to abolish the evils of drink. ►

"See Here, Tockstein, We Need You in Our Business"

How a Patriotic Letter Carrier Came to be Deluged with Fine Business Offers

In Fresno, California, there is a wide-awake young man named Tockstein. Until recently, he wore the blue-gray uniform of the Post Office and delivered letters for Uncle Sam. He was ambitious, and he knew that to get on he must not look for aid outside himself but within.

He had very little time and he was always very tired when he was through with his day's work. But he found a way—and that way is open to you too. The first result of his new way was that he sold 37,744 thrift stamps in one day—breaking all records—simply because he had learned a new way to do the work of three people in one short day without getting tired.

And the next result was that because of his record-breaking feat, he has had offer after offer from responsible business houses at a big increase in salary. He hasn't decided yet which to take—they are all so good.

Now what he did was simple. He sent a coupon like the one at the bottom of this page for

A late-19th-century postcard depicting the "typical" Jew, a merchant with a hooked nose, ingratiating manners, and a cunning look. The other illustration is an early-20th-century ad showing that proverbially ambitious Jews may be expected to have an honorable future, with gentile support.

181

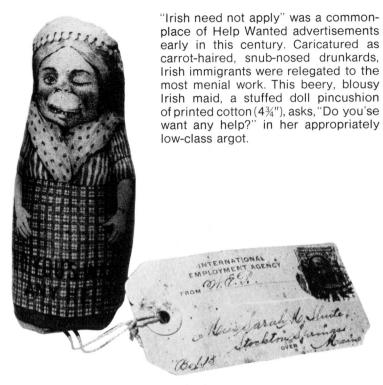

"Irish need not apply" was a commonplace of Help Wanted advertisements early in this century. Caricatured as carrot-haired, snub-nosed drunkards, Irish immigrants were relegated to the most menial work. This beery, blousy Irish maid, a stuffed doll pincushion of printed cotton (4¾"), asks, "Do you'se want any help?" in her appropriately low-class argot.

The indigenous hula dancers of Hawaii wear traditional skirts made of ti leaves. The kitschy version, for the benefit of tourists, is made of glittering and revealing cellophane, no more authentic than the toenail polish.

Racism for fun and profit—but even kitsch makes some progress. This early-20th-century soft-soap advertisement represents an advance over the only-good-Indians-are-dead-Indians popular attitude of earlier generations.

A recent photograph of a South Dakota Indian reservation, where How Kola and performing Indians are available for the Yankee dollar.

Amos 'n' Andy, a tremendously popular radio program that spanned three decades, personified black stereotypes—lovable incompetents who mangled the language ("I'se regusted"). As in minstrel shows, the characters were played by white performers: Freeman Gosden ("Amos") and Charles Correll ("Andy"). (7½")

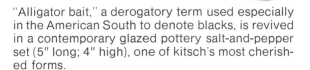

"Alligator bait," a derogatory term used especially in the American South to denote blacks, is revived in a contemporary glazed pottery salt-and-pepper set (5" long; 4" high), one of kitsch's most cherished forms.

Chinese laborers were imported into America in large numbers during the building of the transcontinental railroads. By the end of that era, they had become, in kitsch concept, either operators of opium dens or laundrymen. These late-19th-century advertising cards portray Chinese in the latter rôle. In one, the soap product makes their otherwise subhuman existence downright joyful. The other, bearing the caption "No more washee washee, Melican man wear celluloid collar and cuff," promises fulfillment of white Americans' undisguised hopes that the Chinese, finally put out of work, would climb into their washtubs and go back to where they came from.

Contrasting graduation cards help perpetuate culturally assigned rôles. The male, a young Colossus, stands astride the world, prepared to fulfill his useful destiny. The female's "specialness," unspecified, consists of desirable prettiness.

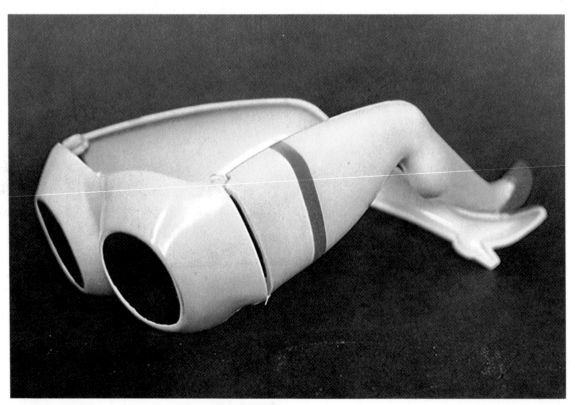

Kooky sunglasses can be more than merely schlock-for-laughs. This pair displays woman as the inevitable sex object, a willing participant in cunnilingus.

CHAPTER 12

Superkitsch
The worst of everything

In every skill and creative art, there are accomplishments that stand out to earn for themselves a place in a pantheon of the incomparable. For supreme achievement in the realm of bad taste, the following nominations are made to the Kitsch Hall of Dubious Fame.

All at sea. In this painted white metal mantel clock of the 1930s (11¾"x13"), the symbolic figure of Uncle Sam is made three-dimensional; but the real person, Franklin D. Roosevelt, is rendered as a mere portrait. And nobody is at the wheel of the Ship of State. Although the metaphor of steering is rendered literally, the American bald eagle has become stylized and sea-going. The nation's guiding star conveniently sheds light on this political extravaganza. But what is a clock doing amid all this delightfully naive, patriotic claptrap?

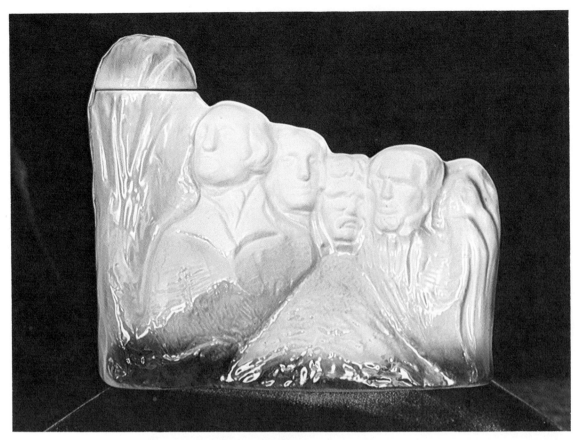

As though Mount Rushmore weren't kitschy enough, a distiller has turned that monster monument into an irridescent bourbon bottle (7½"x9").

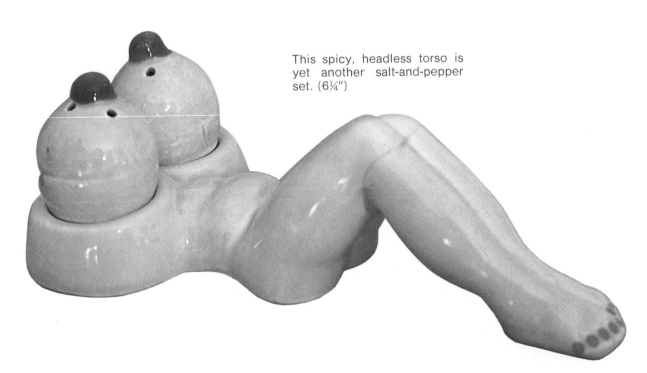

This spicy, headless torso is yet another salt-and-pepper set. (6¼")

Tea pours from under the lady's hoop skirt, as well as from the car radiator in these amusing, but infelicitous, teapots (7½"; 4") from the 1930s.

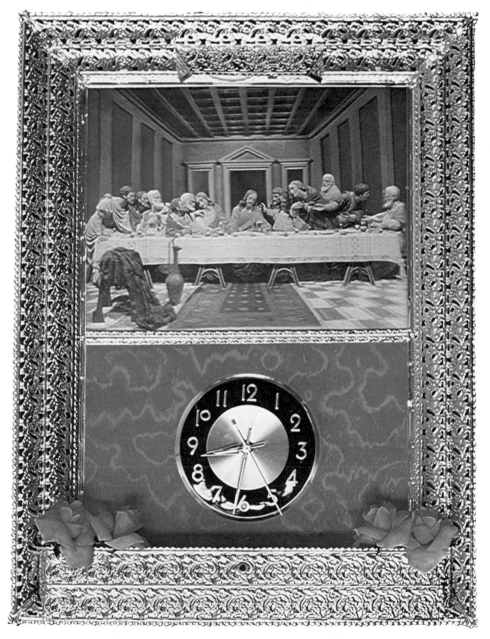

Three-dimensional photography, an Oriental carpet on the floor, and a pile of guests' cloaks dress up *The Last Supper.* The electric clock above a plastic rose garden assures promptness at mealtime. (An alternate model of this religio-utilitarian mishmash replaces the red velvet with a mirror.) (21"x28½")

Edward Savage's painting of 1796, *Liberty. In the form of the Goddess of Youth: giving Support to the Bald Eagle,* inspired numerous copies, including this reverse painting on glass (15½"x23¾"). The goddess, in an international gesture, tramples beneath her foot the key to the Bastille and the star of the Order of the Garter, both symbols of tyranny.

"Intercultural supportive overkill" is the phrase that best describes the massive caryatids (Ancient Greece) of this carport at the Kapok Tree (Indonesia) Inn, Madeira Beach, Florida.

A gratuitous plug for the light of Freedom.

Nobody who heard Florence Foster Jenkins (1868-1944) sing is likely to forget the experience. Possessed of unearthly costumes and an ungodly voice, Madame Jenkins for decades gave annual recitals, in New York and Newport, to an ever-expanding coterie that included Katherine Cornell, Lily Pons, and Cole Porter. She assaulted classics of the coloratura repertoire—the Bell Song from *Lakmé* and the Queen of the Night aria from *The Magic Flute,* for example—with her own tempos, skipping passages at will and rarely hitting a right note. By the time she felt ready (at the age of 76) for her Carnegie Hall debut, she had become legendary, and 2,000 disappointed fans had to be turned away from the packed house. She never suspected the true nature of the unalloyed pleasure she gave her cheering audiences. But with her usual supreme self-confidence, she would not be in the least surprised to learn that her recordings are treasured collector's items among cognoscenti of the unique in vocal art.

A hauntingly majestic Easter Island monolith and, once again, the Great Sphinx turn up at Panama City Beach, Florida, as obstacles for miniature Goofy Golf.

Ouch! This brass ashtray (6″) is a painful example of Victorian kitsch.

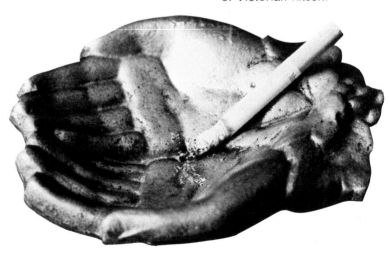

Spin the propellor of this chrome cigarette lighter of the 1930s (3"x6"x5") and the cockpit bursts into flame. Hardly an ideal bon voyage gift.

Theda Bara (1890-1955) was the first and kitschiest of the Hollywood vamps. She slithered and slinked her way through forty movies such as *A Fool There Was* ("Kiss Me, My Fool!"), *Du Barry, Salome,* between 1914 and 1918, before audiences began to laugh. In this still from *Cleopatra* (1918), Bara is more butterfly of the old Bijou than serpent of old Nile.

These flesh-colored candles (2½") and bobbing, wind-up breast of spongy styrofoam (3¾") merit the booby prize for Kinky Kitsch.

The Graham Glass house, built in Portland, Oregon, in the 1880s, was a pinnacle of Victorian ostentation.

AMERICA ON ITS KNEES:

☆ ☆ ☆ not beaten there by the hammer & sickle, but FREELY, INTELLIGENTLY, RESPONSIBLY, CONFIDENTLY, POWERFULLY. America now knows it can destroy communism & win the battle for peace. We need fear nothing or no one...   ...except GOD.

OUR FATHER IN HEAVEN:

WE PRAY that YOU save us from *ourselves*.

The world that YOU have made for us, to live in peace,
    we have made into an armed camp.
    We live in fear of war to come.

We are afraid of "the terror that flies by
    night, and the arrow that flies by day,
    the pestilence that walks in darkness
    and the destruction that wastes at noon-day."

We have turned from YOU to go our selfish way.
    We have broken YOUR commandments
    and denied YOUR truth. We have left YOUR altars
    to serve the false gods of money and pleasure and power.

FORGIVE US AND HELP US

Now, darkness gathers around us and we are confused
    in all our counsels. Losing faith in YOU,
    we lose faith in ourselves.

Inspire us with wisdom, all of us of every color, race and creed,
    to use our wealth, our strength to help our brother,
    instead of destroying him.

Help us to do YOUR will as it is done in heaven
    and to be worthy of YOUR promise of peace on earth.

Fill us with new faith, new strength and new courage,
    that we may win the Battle for Peace.

Be swift to save us,   *dear God,*
    before the darkness falls ★ ☆ ★

FROM "THE BATTLE FOR PEACE" an address by CONRAD N. HILTON

Uncle Sam's prayer is a hypocritical plea for peace, disguising a call to hatred. On view at the Beverly Hilton, Los Angeles, the prayer was written by Conrad Hilton, founding father of the hotel chain, in consultation with Norman Vincent Peale and Fulton Oursler, the author of *The Greatest Story Ever Told.*

If Miss Liberty's night light and thermometer (8") were full size, each of them would be 150 feet high. The cord would stretch about half a mile into the Atlantic Ocean.

They're neither from Ruritania nor from *Duck Soup;* they're the uniforms of the White House guards that made a brief appearance during the Nixon administration, before being laughed into mothballs. The gentleman with the monocle is Erich von Stroheim, the silent-movie "heavy" and director, in *Foolish Wives* (1921). His penchant for fancy military regalia would have earned him the rank of generalissimo in the White House guard.

In 1876, when lawmen tracked down the notorious Younger gang of bank and train robbers in Northfield, Minnesota, thousands of thrill-seekers flocked to see the jailed survivors. Admiring ladies brought the outlaws gifts of flowers, food, and cigars. Local exploiters photographed the captors and the desperadoes—including three bare-chested dead ones—and sold 50,000 copies of this gory commemorative souvenir card.

Any place but here. Any time but now. In Southern California, the land of eternal kitsch, stands this mobile home facsimile of an Egyptian tomb *(top)*. The gleaming towers of Ruidoso, New Mexico *(below)*, beckon to those who yearn for a return to the days of King Arthur and fairy-tale lands of perpetual childhood.

Above: "A genuine waterwheel propels life-like figurines in and out of a miniature mill structure" is how the Madonna Inn, in San Luis Obispo, Calif., describes the Old Mill Room. The chamber offers all the kitsch charm of a giant cuckoo clock. *Below:* The famed Inn also provides this bathroom for the effete caveperson who demands stained-glass windows and gilt-flower lighting fixtures.

The impossible dream realized at last. The only way to enter the personalized "contemplative environment" is by means of a specially notched sterling silver tag. This egg-world has sliding panels to permit a one-way view of the actual world or superimposed film of the dream-world of one's choice, accompanied by background music or "canned" sounds of nature. Soundproofed artificial worlds for the totally alienated, these custom-made wombs begin at $80,000.

In September 1973, as he lay dying of cancer in New York's Columbus Hospital, Candy Darling (né James Slattery, Jr.), one of Andy Warhol's transvestite "Superstars," summoned a photographer for this bizarre, yet strangely moving "farewell to my friends." Although the portrait is tastelessly self-exploitative, its quiet, resigned mood suggests a toughness of spirit wholly at odds with a first impression of sentimental softness. The following March, Candy Darling, at the age of 26, died, leaving behind this unforgettable instance of gloriously transcendent Superkitsch.

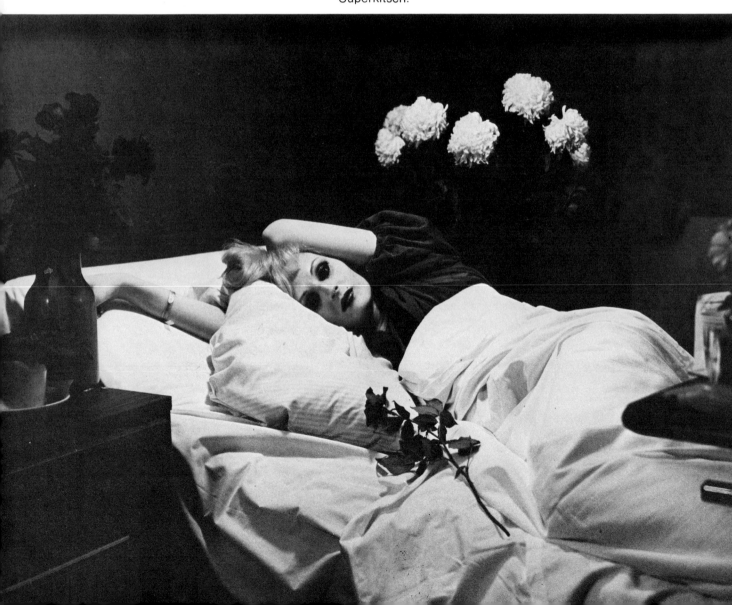

This patriotic icon is a ceramic salt-and-pepper set (4"). The pepper comes from the back of the rocker; and the salt, from holes in President Kennedy's head.

Bibliography

Dorfles, Gillo. *Kitsch: The World of Bad Taste.* New York: Universe Books, 1969. An informative, at times abstruse, illustrated collection of essays on the topography of kitsch, principally European.

Haden-Guest, Anthony. *The Paradise Program: Travels through Muzak, Hilton, Coca-Cola, Texaco, Walt Disney, and other World Empires.* New York: Morrow, 1973. Issued in Great Britain as *Down the Programmed Rabbit Hole: Travels through Muzak, Hilton, Coca-Cola, Walt Disney and other World Empires.* London: Hart-Davis, MacGibbon, 1972. A British writer's witty, often scathing, impressions of America's "computerized" mass culture.

Price, Roger. *The Great Roob Revolution.* New York: Random House, 1970. An amusing, occasionally irascible, examination of contemporary American mores and taste.

Rosenberg, Bernard, and White, David Manning (eds.). *Mass Culture: The Popular Arts in America.* New York: Free Press, 1957. A compilation of essays by outstanding art and literary critics, social scientists, and journalists presenting "pro" and "con" views. Includes three seminal essays on kitsch: "Avant-Garde and Kitsch," by Clement Greenberg, "A Theory of Mass Culture," by Dwight MacDonald, and "Of Happiness and Despair We Have No Measure," by Ernest van den Haag.

——— *Mass Culture Revisited.* New York: Van Nostrand Reinhold, 1971. A contemporary collection of essays, again representing a balanced point of view.

Rosenberg, Harold. *The Tradition of the New.* New York: Horizon Press, 1959. The chapter entitled "Pop Culture: Kitsch Criticism" discusses Rosenberg and White's *Mass Culture.*

Schrank, Jeffrey. "Kitsch: A Guided Tour." *Media & Methods,* January 1973, p. 32. A lively and informative illustrated article on contemporary American kitsch.

Sternberg, Jacques. *Kitsch.* Edited by Marina Henderson. New York: St. Martin's Press, 1972. An illustrated historical and international survey, concentrating on sexual kitsch.

Suares, Jean-Claude. "A Designer's Guide to Schlock, Camp & Kitsch—and the Taste of Things to Come." *Print,* January/February 1975, pp. 25-35. International in scope, this profusely illustrated article shows the distinction and mutation between levels of bad taste.

The Wichita Art Museum has published "Kitsch: The Grotesque Around Us," an illustrated brochure, in conjunction with a 1970-71 traveling exhibition, organized by the Wichita Art Museum and its then director, Jan Ernst Adlmann.

Acknowledgments

The author wishes to thank the following for their expert assistance in creating this book: Karen Tobias, who researched many of the illustrations; Ihor B. Lysak, who photographed many of the objects; and Muriel T. Barron, George Haimsohn, Stan Landsman, Donald McQuade, Ed Plunkett, staff members of The Free Library of Philadelphia, and Jan Ernst Adlmann, director of the Long Beach Museum of Art, Long Beach, California, who offered helpful suggestions. For the loan of many of the items pictured, he is grateful to the owners of private collections: Carol Wald, Fred Haynes, B. J. Dockweiler, and Susan Kocik, all of New York, and Susan Steckler, of New Jersey; to Phil Balestrino, Dick Dulany, and Fred Haynes of The Pilgrim's Progress Antiques, and to Bob Shulman of Friends & Lovers Antiques, both of New York; to Fran and Steve Gertz of Citybarn Antiques, Brooklyn, and to The Treasure Chest Antiques, Gardiner, Maine. Special thanks to Mary N. Rivers, of Beaufort, South Carolina, who fashioned most of the candles shown in the book.

Most particularly, thanks and deep gratitude are due Hayden Goldberg, wise friend and counselor, who provided invaluable aid in organizing material, and supplied encouragement when it was most needed.

Credits

The pictures in this book were supplied by the author, with the following exceptions:

American Antiquarian Society: 143 top; Brown Brothers: 122, 123 top left, 123 top right, 123 lower right, 132 top, 140 left; Cincinnati Public Library: 64 top, 64 bottom; Cinemabilia: 15 top left, 15 top right, 15 lower right, 19 top right, 51 bottom, 124 top, 124 bottom, 126 bottom, 134 bottom right, 158 bottom, 162 bottom, 164 top, 176 left, 177 top, 177 bottom, 180 top, 191 bottom, 194 bottom; Corn Palace Concessions: 103 bottom; Dover Publications, Inc., New York. From Edmund V. Gillon, Jr.—*Early Illustrations and Visions of American Architecture:* 101 center; Ford Motor Co.: 16; David Gebhard, The Art Galleries, University of California, Santa Barbara: 104 lower right; Harkness Theatre: 108; Peter Hujar: 198 bottom; Hyatt Hotels: 101 left; Kennedy Center: 104 top; Lady Madonna Maternity Boutique: 161 right; Library of Congress: 33 top, 33 bottom right, 34 top, 41, 97 bottom; Lois, Holland & Callaway: 86 bottom; Miami Metro Department of Publicity and Tourism: 95 bottom; Minnesota Historical Society: 195; Hugh Morrow: 34 bottom; Movie Star News: 49, 51 top; Museum of the City of New York: 13 top; Photo by Byron—the Byron Collection: 141 bottom; NCR Corporation: 123 lower left; Neiman-Marcus: 142 top, 142 bottom, 198 top; New York Historical Society: 109 top; New York Public Library: 18, 42 bottom, 43 top, 79 top left, 79 top right, 79 bottom, 83 top, 85 right, 175 bottom left; *The New York Times*/Ruth Rejnis: 197 top; Oregon Historical Society: 192 bottom; Harry T. Peters, Jr., Collection: 115; Photo Archives: 24, 25, 50 top, 50 bottom, 58 top, 125 center, 126 top, 129 bottom, 134 top left, 134 top right, 140 bottom right, 174 bottom, 175 top; Photo Archives/© Walt Disney Productions: 107; Eric Pollitzer/Leo Castelli Gallery: 110 center; The Preservation Society of Newport County: 95 center right; Virginia State Library: 33; San Simeon: 96 top left, 96 bottom left; Smithsonian Institution: 109 bottom, 188 top; UPI: 29, 35 top, 35 center, 35 bottom, 36 top, 43 bottom right, 43 bottom left, 47 top right, 47 bottom, 48 top, 48 bottom left, 54 top, 54 center, 54 bottom, 57 top right, 57 left, 57 bottom right, 59 top, 59 bottom right, 91 bottom, 96 right, 97 top right, 98 top left, 98 right, 98 bottom left, 99 top, 99 bottom, 101 top, 102 top, 102 bottom, 103 top, 104 bottom left, 119 bottom, 125 top, 125 bottom, 127 top right, 127 center, 128 top, 128 bottom, 131 top, 131 left, 131 bottom, 132 bottom, 133 top, 133 center, 134 bottom left, 138 left, 146 top, 146 bottom right, 146 bottom left, 150 top, 152 top left, 156 top, 156 bottom, 157 top, 157 bottom right, 157 bottom left, 158 top, 160 left, 164 bottom, 169 bottom, 176 right, 182 top left, 194 top; UPI/© Walt Disney Productions: 40; William Webb: 197 bottom; The Wichita Art Museum. From exhibition *Kitsch: The Grotesque Around Us:* 53 bottom right, 58 bottom right, 67 right, 72 top right, 141 right; Grant Wood, *American Gothic*, Courtesy of the Art Institute of Chicago: 111 bottom; Woodfin Camp and Associates—Thomas Höpker Photo: 139 right; Tim Eagen Photo: 182 bottom.

"Vagabond's House." Reprinted by permission of DODD, MEAD & COMPANY, INC. from VAGABOND'S HOUSE by Don Blanding. Copyright 1928, 1956 by Don Blanding.

The Author

As a child, Curtis F. Brown was presented with a terrifyingly large, but fascinating, cast-iron grasshopper pull toy (long since disappeared). Since then, he has purposely acquired similar items of questionable use and attractiveness, many of which are pictured in *Star-Spangled Kitsch*. Mr. Brown also collects what he supposes are non-kitsch antiques, including American pressed glass and American historical views on Staffordshire china.

The author of *Ingrid Bergman*, a volume in the Pyramid Illustrated History of the Movies, and a contributor to *The Movie Buff's Book*, edited by Ted Sennett, Mr. Brown was born in Cambridge, Mass., and educated at Tufts and Columbia universities. A former faculty member of Tufts University and Drexel University, literary editor and writer for CBS Records, and copywriter for two major New York publishing houses, he is currently an administrative assistant at the City University of New York. He lives in a restored 1840 town house in Brooklyn.